Chasing the Wind

Chasing the Wind

*Christianity and the Quest for
the Life Worth Living*

Neil H. Williams

WIPF & STOCK · Eugene, Oregon

CHASING THE WIND
Christianity and the Quest for the Life Worth Living

Copyright © 2021 Neil H. Williams. All rights reserved. Except for brief quotations in critical publications or reviews, no part of this book may be reproduced in any manner without prior written permission from the publisher. Write: Permissions, Wipf and Stock Publishers, 199 W. 8th Ave., Suite 3, Eugene, OR 97401.

Wipf & Stock
An Imprint of Wipf and Stock Publishers
199 W. 8th Ave., Suite 3
Eugene, OR 97401

www.wipfandstock.com

PAPERBACK ISBN: 978-1-6667-1816-4
HARDCOVER ISBN: 978-1-6667-1817-1
EBOOK ISBN: 978-1-6667-1818-8

11/03/21

Unless otherwise indicated, Scripture quotations are from New Revised Standard Version Bible, copyright © 1989 National Council of the Churches of Christ in the United States of America. Used by permission. All rights reserved worldwide.

For Matthew and Nathan

Contents

Introduction | 1

Chapter 1 **Chaos Tales: A Disrupted Life** | 10
Disruption and the art of maneuver   12
Relationships disrupt   18
When God shows up   22
The easiest person to fool   24

Chapter 2 **Welcome to the Real World: An Examined Life** | 27
An examined life   27
How to be right and look good   32
Relational failure   37
    Relationships as reality   40
    Legal systems   44
    Emergent properties of relational failure   47
    The Parable of the Prodigal Son   48
Repentance, forgiveness, and the life worth living   51
    Repentance   51
    Forgiveness   57

Chapter 3 **Stories and Games: A Fun Life** | 62
The games we play   63
    The prisoner's dilemma: defect or cooperate?   64
    Infinite games   67
The stories we tell   69
    Once upon a time, there was a great king . . .   69
    Stories of science   72
    Bible stories   79
    Theological stories   89

Chapter 4   **Transforming Stories: A Faithful Life** | 95
          Don't fiddle with my favorite story!   95
          Transforming stories   98
              Transforming Christian stories   100
          A relational test   111
          Jonah's dilemma (Is faith a virtue?)   119

Chapter 5   **Insiders and Outsiders: A Just Life** | 125
          The gods must be crazy   125
              The bio-cultural study of religion   128
          Exclusive clubs: the secret requirement for membership   133
          The seeds of dissolution   137
          Death as a way to life   140
          A new being human   144

End Notes | 153
Bibliography | 161

Introduction

When Socrates said, "an unexamined life is not worth living,"[1] he set before us a quest that requires some questioning, investigation, and reflection. What is a worthwhile life? Who gets to decide what it is? And why make "an examined life" central to this quest?

For many philosophers, the life worth living is a particular kind of life—a good life. This good life isn't a life that pursues all the "goods" and "goodies," but is a right kind of life—a reasonable and flourishing life, a virtuous and just life, an honest and wise life. It is a skeptical life that questions everything, including inquiring of ourselves and our actions.

What does it mean to live a good life when we face climate catastrophe, loss of biodiversity, illegal trade, habitat loss, poaching, pollutants, depleted rainforests and coral reefs, and some scientists thinking that we are on the verge of a mass extinction event?

What does it mean to live the good life when the rich gain more and the poor struggle to survive, when the actions of a few deprive many from a fulfilled life?

What does it mean to live a good life, now that in this stage of our evolutionary history, human societies comprise more than just small primitive clans?

What does it mean to live the good life when our world today still struggles with religion-inspired ignorance, violence, and fanaticism? When individuals and groups still promote xenophobia, misogyny, and racism?

What does it mean to live a good life when governments trample human rights, violate their citizens' privacy, and engage in torture, extrajudicial killings, and aggressive wars?

It's a tall order to find satisfactory answers to such questions. Even if we figure out some answers as to a worthwhile life, it is probable that we are not living this life to the fullest, and thus we face the difficulty of changing the way we live. If we arrive at some answers, what will inspire us to live in a new way?

Our survival and flourishing depend on change. The truism "adapt or die" applies to all species, including our own. Humans, however, need more than biological adaptation to survive and prosper. Our social evolution and ability to transmit our cultures and experiences across generations provide us with further opportunities for change. But with our population numbers, violent coalitions, environmental exploitation, and multiple inequities—between poor and rich, female and male, black and white, LGBTQ and straight/cisgender—we face substantial difficulties. Without change, we are stuck like Sisyphus,[2] ever to repeat our failures and mistakes, unable to learn and grow. Change requires considerable resources—mental effort, courage, self-knowledge, ethical direction, and inspiration. Thus, New Year's resolutions often have the same dreary flavor as the year before, and one of the most frequently blurted pieces of relational advice is, "You can't change the other person."

The question of what is a worthwhile life and how we can achieve it is not only the provenance of moral and political philosophy. Every thinking, self-aware person has an interest in this pursuit, including musicians, artists, writers, scientists, psychologists, philosophers, human rights activists, and environmentalists. Each can bring their perspective to the question and offer answers. It's a vast topic that I will narrow down and place in a context with which I am familiar—Christianity.

How might we in the twenty-first century go about discovering what is a worthwhile life—a good, upright, and just life? And once finding some answers, what may provide incentives to live in this way?

Such a broad topic needs focus to save it from nebulous generalizations and endless words.

First, I assume that a worthwhile life is what many philosophers have described as a good and just life. Because power, money, and influence often accumulate at the expense of other people, I am uninterested in what the sadist, psychopath, self-obsessed, power-hungry, or the money-grubbing may think is the "good life," which usually involves manipulating or abusing people, or enraging crowds through powerful forces of tribalism, racism, and misogyny.

Second, I take for granted that whatever this good life may look like, we are not living it to the fullest, and therefore we need ways to talk about mechanisms for change. Through what processes are individuals and communities encouraged and enabled to lead worthwhile lives?

Third, most of us would assume that a good life includes those things that bring us enjoyment, meaning, and purpose. Many activities and pursuits may contribute to the good life: professional accomplishments, a fulfilling career, hobbies, reading, climbing mountains, painting, motorcycling, playing a musical instrument, gardening, or whatever else. For some, their primary goal in life may be to escape poverty or war. For others it may be to travel more, earn a higher salary, have kids, or learn another language.

These all can bring deep satisfaction, intellectual stimulation, and purpose to our lives. And I intend no disparagement of these pursuits. Nevertheless, my interest in the good life is narrower. I am concerned with those relational aspects that are essential, even core, to the good life—relationships that are central to providing fulfillment, meaning, and purpose.

Fourth, I am uninterested in change for the sake of change, and skeptical of the assumption that change is automatically better for human lives. For example, there is the common refrain from Silicon Valley that "we will change the world." Steve Jobs famously recruited the CEO of PepsiCo John Sculley with the words, "Do you want to sell sugared water for the rest of your life? Or do you want to come with me and change the world?" The world has surely changed through technological innovation. But in the end, our technology is a tool that we may use for good or ill. We now have our goods assembled and shipped by factory workers stressed to the limit by meager wages, grueling conditions, and long working hours. 3D printers can manufacture both customized joint replacements and guns. Facebook can connect family and friends, but also upend democratic elections and entrench dictators. Social media can galvanize human rights protests, but also provide a platform to broadcast public beheadings. Apple's "Think different" slogan is great. "Be different" is better.

Often, these "change the world" CEOs trample over many people in bringing this change. A recent example is of Elizabeth Holmes, whose shenanigans were exposed by the Wall Street journalist John Carreyrou, and he tells the sordid tale in *Bad Blood: Secrets and Lies in a Silicon Valley Startup*.[3] Holmes promised to provide a miraculous device named "Edison" that could accomplish a host of blood diagnostics with a finger prick rather than with the dreaded traditional needle. But the device didn't work, never mind that the companies Safeway and Walgreens had already installed it in their stores and were giving people inaccurate blood test results. Once again, Holmes promised to "change the world," a motto that is often used to manipulate and oppress people, something like, "I'm changing the world—so get in line, do what I say, and keep quiet." Holmes is now facing up to twenty years in federal prison.

Fifth, in considering questions about the worthwhile life, we need dialog partners. These may include philosophy, history, science, psychology, music, religion, or art. This book is a conversation with Christianity, although I will touch on other areas. What makes Christianity an interesting partner for me is that (1) I am familiar with its teachings, and (2) Christianity explicitly claims to have answers as to what is a good life.

Nowadays, engagements with Christianity often fall on opposite ends of a spectrum—either that Christianity "poisons everything" and is best consigned to the rubbish dump, or that Christianity is good and humankind's best hope. My approach is more nuanced, and I attempt to consider both the good and bad.

In summary, this book is a dialog between these two questions: What is a good life, and how does Christianity help or hinder such a life?

* * *

We will engage with Christianity as it relates to the life worth living. Christianity claims to provide answers to the question of what is the good life. In addition, it claims to provide the motivation and ability to achieve such a life. In short, Christianity claims to be transformative. It claims to reconcile people and to provide the direction and power to live a good life—a life that is honest, just, and loving.

One immediate problem is that these claims are not self-evident. When thinking about the history of the church, people often think of the Crusades, religious wars, Inquisition, witch hunts, heretic burnings, persecutions of heathen, pogroms against Jews, obscene collections of wealth, abuse of power, marginalization of women, forgiving sins or granting freedom from purgatory for cash, inciting anti-gay laws and violence, child abuse scandals, or the election of Donald Trump in 2016. When considering human rights, people usually don't first imagine a multitude of churches at the forefront of rights for slaves, blacks, women, children, or the LGBTQ community. When considering the environment, churches are often low on the list of those groups sounding the alarm, and Christians often disparage the scientific consensus. And when thinking about power and its abuse, people often remember the church's collusion with empires—Roman, Spanish, British, and American—and that systemic evils such as manifest destiny and apartheid were inextricably entwined with Christianity.

Do Christians have demonstrably better relationships (for example, in their marriages or with people outside their group) than non-believers or believers in other religions?[4] Is there evidence that Christians are more likely to "love their neighbor" or to "speak the truth"? Or is Freud's opinion correct in *The Future of an Illusion*, where he said, "Where questions of religion are concerned people are guilty of every kind of insincerity and intellectual misdemeanor."[5] Do clergy exhibit higher moral standards? For many outside the church, the horrific child abuse scandal has evaporated any last vestige of the church's moral conduct, compass, or authority.

Consider, for example, the subject of violence—its causes and decline. Harvard cognitive psychologist Steven Pinker in *The Better Angels of Our Nature: Why Violence has Declined* has convincingly argued for the counterintuitive conclusion that violence has declined over time. War, genocide, crime, human sacrifice, slavery, torture, cruelty, racism, homophobia, homicide, abuse of women, dueling, child abuse, and corporal punishment have all declined in scientifically measurable ways. But in analyzing the reasons for this decline—which include female empowerment, better education, international trade, and even the reading of fiction—Pinker notes that religion is *not* one of the forces that has led to the decline in violence.[6] Some people have used religion for good, others for evil, but overall, religion is not a force for tempering violence. In addition, Pinker writes that "the Abrahamic religions ratified some of our worst instincts with laws and beliefs that have encouraged violence for millennia: the demonization of infidels, the ownership of women, the sinfulness of children, the abomination of homosexuality, the dominion over animals and denial of them of souls."[7]

There are counterexamples. Of course, many Christians lead upright lives and aspire to live the good life. Christian stories have encouraged many to live worthwhile lives and have inspired great art, music, science, and literature. Christians have founded orphanages, hospitals, homeless shelters, educational institutions, organizations to combat human trafficking, and charitable organizations. Christian leaders, such as Desmond Tutu and Martin Luther King Jr., have led movements against racism. And many churches help the disadvantaged in their communities. But we cannot say that these charitable actions balance out the bad without minimizing the vast atrocities committed in the name of Christianity. Let's just say at the outset that Christianity has an ambiguous, troubled, and perplexing relationship with the good life.

Christianity's authoritative texts reflect this troublesome duality. For example, we have Paul's statement in 1 Corinthians 13: 4–6: "Love is patient; love is kind; love is not envious or boastful or arrogant or rude. It does not insist on its own way; it is not irritable or resentful; it does not rejoice in wrongdoing, but rejoices in the truth"—a beautiful passage often read at weddings and one that few outside Christianity would have any objection to. Contrast this with another famous passage in Numbers 31 where God commands Moses to wage war against the Midianites. Following God's directive, the Israelites slaughter every adult male and the kings of Midian. If that isn't terrible enough, the Israelites also capture all the women and children, plunder their possessions, and burn their towns. Worse still, Moses orders the Israelites to kill all the young boys and all the women who have slept with a man. The Israelites, however, could keep all the virgins for themselves. Here we have divinely authorized war, genocide, looting, indiscriminate slaughter, capture of women during war, rape, and the needless destruction of property. Thankfully, given the lack of historical evidence for the Conquest of Canaan, these events and others like it most probably didn't happen as described. But they are still part of Christian stories, and most explanations today require some deft theological gymnastics.

We also see this duality in disagreements among Christians themselves over the good life. There are and have been Christians for and against apartheid, slavery, gay marriage, gun control, human rights for women, the findings of modern science, the waging of aggressive war, strict environmental controls, decriminalization of drug use, stem cell research, and birth control. On any important ethical topic today, we have diverse Christian voices. We have people such as Desmond Tutu, whose Christianity is a driving force for his humanitarianism, but we have others whose Christianity inspired them to support segregation. For every kindly bishop Muriel (Hugo's *Les Misérables*) we can find a Grand Inquisitor (Dostoyevsky's *The Brothers Karamazov*). Christians cannot agree among themselves what is a worthwhile life and haven't arrived at any unanimous conclusions on the major issues of our time. Ask Christians about their views on women, gays, raising children, science, politics, psychology, ethics, philosophy—you will get a multitude of different answers.

Christianity is as diverse as humanity itself—from the psychopathic to the altruistic, and everything in between. That Christianity has been involved in much mischief, violence, and evil is beyond dispute. Thus, Christianity has an ambiguous relationship with the good life. On the one hand, the central message of Christianity is about love and transformation. The stories of Christianity proliferate with tales of God reconciling the world, offering salvation (however it is understood), and highlighting that love is the greatest virtue that fulfills all that God requires. Christianity promises new life, which is presumably better than the old one. Given its claims, we should expect Christianity over these past two thousand years to have remarkable and concrete results. On the other hand, Christianity is mired in structures, belief systems, teaching, and behavior that often decisively undermine relationships.

* * *

Throughout this book, I will usually refer to Christianity in the singular for convenience. Although today there are some forty thousand denominations within Christianity, it is still possible to speak in the singular. There have always been multiple forms of Christianity, even from its earliest beginnings. Perhaps the only unifying characteristic is that all these groups claim to follow Jesus of Nazareth. I think of Christianity as I think of Africa. As Africa is my birthplace, Christianity is my religious family of origin. Africa is divided but can be viewed as a singular continent. Africa has fifty-four countries, approximately two thousand languages, and over three thousand ethnic groups. And within each national border are many coalitions, some vehemently opposed to each other. Africa has some beautiful places, some that are crazy, and some violent sections where you wouldn't travel without armed escort. Such is the continent of Christianity.

In addition, it is sometimes helpful to distinguish between "Christianity," "church," and "Christians." The first is a system of thought, the second a social organization, and the third a self-designation adopted by individuals. So, for example, a critique against what the church did in a particular time and culture may not necessarily be a critique against Christianity—whose central values and teaching may in fact critique the church. But for convenience I will often use the word "Christianity" to include all three—Christians, churches, and Christian teaching—and only draw distinctions when necessary.

* * *

The title *Chasing the Wind* is a play on three meanings. First is the idea that the quest for the good life is elusive and has no conclusive answers. At no point will we reach the end of the journey. What Socrates thought was the good life will differ from ours. The quest was different in the past and will be in the future. Answers change over time and there are no twelve or fifty steps to the good life. One hundred years from now, many of our ideas will seem quaint or even immoral. Others will have different ideas of what is a worthwhile life from what I suggest. There is no single path to a flourishing human life. But there are common elements. The quest is like trying to understand the weather. Meteorologists may discern patterns and general themes but can be surprised by unexpected weather. Even if they consider all the pressure systems and other contributing factors to the weather, including ocean currents, geology, glaciers, sunspots, or even our position in the galaxy, there is always something changing or some knowledge out of reach.

Second, in the Christian tradition, the Spirit of God is associated with the wind—who was over the chaotic waters at creation (Gen 1:2) and who is like the wind that goes wherever it pleases (John 3:8). In this sense, Christians are seeking after the Spirit of God, whom they believe leads and empowers people to live worthwhile lives.

Third, given the considerable evidence of the harm done in the name of Christianity, there are at least some Christian approaches that are foolish, toxic, or deadly. In this sense, some forms of Christianity are indeed chasing the wind in the sense that they promote social discord and undermine the life worth living.

* * *

Finally, some remarks about my approach. This is a critical-sympathetic interaction with Christianity. I can imagine that some readers will think that I have grossly erred on the critical side, while others will think that I have been far too sympathetic. But I have attempted to be fair and to acknowledge both the good and bad.

My experience within Christianity includes undergraduate, masters, and doctorate degrees in theology. I was an ordained pastor, taught theology at a college, published theological literature, and helped train pastors for ministry. I am well acquainted with Christian thinking, stories, arguments, and beliefs.

In the interests of clarity, my position today is that I still view Christianity as having some remarkable stories and some utility, but I no longer believe or accept that there is a supernatural agent behind these stories. Neither do I think that belief in the supernatural is a requirement to live or justify a good life. Although this is not a book on why I left Christianity, some of my reasons will become apparent—including scientific, ethical, personal, philosophical, and even biblical and theological reasons.

Here I am concerned with the questions: In what ways does Christianity hinder or help the good life? Are there versions of Christianity that help toward living a good life? Do even the most enlightened forms of Christianity still hinder the worthwhile life because they trap people in tribal and magical thinking, all the while propping up harmful forms of Christianity? And do answers also depend on the individual person? Do good people use the Bible in good ways, and awful people use it for evil?

With some 2.4 billion adherents, we all have a personal stake in how Christians act in this world. Given the history of the church, some forms of

Christianity undoubtedly undermine the good life. We will address these cases and consider how Christianity itself may continue to transform.

Since the dawn of the written word, and probably much longer, humans have wondered what is a worthwhile life and how to strive toward it. Every day we are reminded how much human beings and their behavior still need transformation—from violence, greed, exclusion, power struggles, and exploitation.

So now on to considering a worthwhile life and how we can work towards it—while reflecting on and engaging with Christianity's claim to engender this good life through its teaching and practice. We start at the beginning with how we may notice a need for change. Where are we as individuals or as a community not living the good life to its fullest?

Chapter 1

Chaos Tales: A Disrupted Life

It is not the strongest of the species that survives, nor the most intelligent that survives. It is the one that is most adaptable to change.

—Darwin

Sweet are the uses of adversity,
Which, like the toad, ugly and venomous,
Wears yet a precious jewel in his head;
And this is our life, exempt from public haunt,
Finds tongues in trees, books in the running brooks,
Sermons in stones, and good in everything.

—Shakespeare, *As You Like It*, 2.1.12-17

Time's glory is to calm contending kings,
To unmask falsehood, and bring truth to light,
To stamp the seal of time in aged things,
To wake the morn, and sentinel the night,
To wrong the wronger till he render right.

—Shakespeare, *The Rape of Lucrece*, l. 941

My flight was leaving at 8:00 a.m. and I had arrived at the Philadelphia International Airport with plenty of time to spare. Queues are a common grumbling point and to be on time for a morning flight required rising far too early. Fortunately, I found a shorter line for an automatic check-in console, where you can easily swipe your credit card and have a boarding pass issued. But when my turn came, it didn't work. I swiped a few more times and got the same message: "Unable to issue a boarding pass at this time." Stupid machine, I thought. Now I must get into another line—at the back—to speak to a living soul. After half an hour of waiting, I handed my ticket information to the clerk and subtly mentioned that their machines were messed up. She replied, "Ah, Mr. Williams, do you know your ticket is for the flight leaving at 8:00 *p.m.*?" I had arrived twelve hours early.

My troubles didn't end there. Almost immediately, I recalled a meeting a few days before. A colleague relayed how he had recently arrived at the airport to take a flight, only to find that he had arrived on the wrong day. Everyone laughed, including me. But I thought to myself, "What an idiot! What are calendars for? Next time check your ticket and make sure that you have the right time and day."

Psychologists speak of cognitive dissonance to explain a variety of behaviors, including self-justification. Dissonance occurs when the reality confronting us undermines deep-seated beliefs, ideas, and cherished views of ourselves. I see myself as intelligent, timely, and competent enough to arrive at the airport at the correct time. So much so that I will swiftly condemn someone who arrived on the wrong day. I had thrown out the boomerang of judgment and it had swiftly returned to clobber me on the head. I arrived at the wrong time and now I remember what I usually think of people who make mistakes like this.

Events like this are disorientating—when reality pulls the rug from under us, when we temporarily lose our balance, when we grab for the nearest railing or excuse. Our first inclination is to regain our balance and carry on, hoping no one noticed our slip. But what if we paused, were more attentive, and slower to shake off such situations? We would have in our grasp a key element in pursuing the good life. Disruptive moments such as these alert us to something that is amiss and provide an opportunity for change.

A first, but often neglected, step toward the good life is considering how we as individuals, communities, or nations can discover hindrances to living worthwhile lives. Knowing where we need to change, however, is much harder than it sounds. We often live with a lack of self-awareness, unaware of our relational failure, and even when we have a vague cognizance that something is wrong, we often have little compulsion or motivation to change. In such cases, we need a disruptive splash of ice water to wake us up to reality.

Disruption and the art of maneuver

The concept of disruption is prized in another field—maneuver warfare theory—and provides an illustration for my point.[8] Disruption as a prime tactic in war has been highly valued for at least two and a half millennia, going back to when the Chinese general Sun Tzu wrote in *The Art of War* that the best military leader wins the battle not by fighting but by out-maneuvering and disrupting the enemy.[9] In maneuver-warfare theory, the idea is to defeat your enemy in the quickest and most efficient way, preferably without even fighting. The art of maneuver-warfare is to render the strength of your opponent irrelevant, to throw them off balance, to neutralize or destroy their center of gravity. And this is done through disruption.

In World War II, when Germany planned to invade France, the Nazis faced the substantial and sophisticated fortified barrier the French had erected on their border with Germany—the Maginot Line. This snake of concrete, steel, turrets, tunnels, and guns once stretched from the Swiss border to Luxembourg.[10] Remnants of this massive barrier survive today. The Maginot Line was a marvel of early-twentieth-century engineering, designed to smash and repel any German invaders—provided the Germans came that way. Germany had other ideas, ignored France's position of strength, and took a different route through the Low Countries and the unlikely Ardennes forest. General Erich von Manstein, most probably the greatest strategist of the war, with the help of General Heinz Guderian, devised the "sickle cut" plan—one of the most brilliant strategic maneuvers in military history—that cut the Allied forces in two. This disruptive German blitzkrieg outmaneuvered the French and quickly rendered their strength irrelevant. Although France had one of the largest and strongest armies, this disruption, coupled with France's poor communications, poor command and control, indecisive leadership, and a defensive mentality, led to their capitulation in six weeks. In just six weeks, the Germans had achieved what they could not do in World War I in four years of fighting.

The greatest military strategists were all masters of maneuver. From the Carthaginian general Hannibal, who disrupted Roman expectations by leading his army from Spain, crossing the Alps, and onto his famous encirclement of the Roman army at Cannae, to Field Marshall Erwin Rommel, the "Desert Fox," who with limited resources regularly outmaneuvered his enemies. One of his chief opponents, Field Marshall Bernard

Montgomery, observed when speaking of Rommel, "He is best at the spoiling attack; his *forte* is disruption."[11]

In *The Art of Maneuver: Maneuver-Warfare Theory and Airland Battle*, Robert Leonhard illustrates the central place of disruption by examining the biblical story of the clash between David and Goliath.[12] For Leonhard, Goliath is the center of gravity for the Philistine army—the king on the chessboard. He is a towering brute who has equipped himself with imposing armor and weapons. Everything depends on defeating Goliath.

When David takes up the challenge to defeat Goliath, the situation looks bleak. King Saul places his armor on David, to the point where David cannot *move*. Saul ignores maneuver-warfare, because if you cannot move you cannot outmaneuver and disrupt your enemies. And in maneuver-warfare you never try to match your strength with your enemy's—at best that will get you into a prolonged battle of attrition. A quick way to lose the flight would be for David to attempt to match Goliath's strength, height, armor, and weapons.

Instead, David takes off the armor, leaves the sword behind, sprints toward Goliath (another unexpected move), and with his sling and a stone David renders Goliath's strength and weapons irrelevant. The result is the disruption of the Philistine army. David targeted and destroyed their center of gravity, and when the Philistines saw their hero was dead, they turned and ran.

To use a variety of metaphors: disruption rattles our center of gravity. It unhinges the door. It dislocates our hip.[13] It shakes the ground and throws us off balance. Disruption is the arrow through our Achilles' heel, the arrow that targets our critical vulnerabilities.[14] By throwing us off balance, disruption renders our perceived position of strength irrelevant, shifts our view of the world, and gives us an opportunity to see what we were blind to.

Some examples of disruptive situations readily come to mind—job loss, divorce, health collapse, a death in the family, a victim of violent crime, or an addiction exposed. But if we limit our thinking to only these, we lose much of value. Many commonplace occurrences can provide an opportunity to consider our lives and relationships. Some may seem minute or inconsequential—a tip of an iceberg—but indicate a frozen mass underneath.

Disruption can often come from *beneficial situations*—including an unexpected kindness, a sincere apology, an apt question, a pang of conscience, a great joke, a forgiving word, a line in a song. Disruption may arrive while reading a book, listening to a story or a beautiful piece of music, viewing a work of art, falling in love, or tackling a new subject—perhaps an area of literature, philosophy, music, or science that increases our realization of how little we know.

For the few astronauts who have had the opportunity of viewing our earth from outer space, most have experienced disruptive moments. They have seen the earth from a remarkably unfamiliar perspective—with its beauty, life, sacredness, even its frailty and aloneness. Alan Shepard is famous as the first American in orbit and for hitting golf balls on the moon, but he is also to be remembered as the one who wept as he viewed the earth from the moon. From his book *Moon Shot*, we read of him looking back to earth, "'But from here, from the moon,' he spoke quietly to himself, 'it is, in fact, very finite, very fragile . . . so incredibly fragile. That thin, thin atmosphere, the thinnest shell of air hugging the world—it can be blown away so easily! A meteor, a cataclysmic volcano, man's own uncaring outpourings of poison . . .'"[15]

This new perspective gave us the heightened sense that the earth is all we have, that we must take care of it, and that love for the whole earth, including all humans, is paramount. And it led some to say, "What was most significant about the first lunar voyage was not that men set foot on the moon, but that they set eye on the earth."[16] We went to discover the moon, but perhaps the most enduring legacy is that we rediscovered the earth.

Most of us will stay planted on the earth. But, though a distant second, even a photograph of outer space can unsettle us. Carl Sagan and others have remarked that astronomy is a humbling and character-building experience. Try to grasp the size of the universe and brain rivets pop. One of the Hubble Telescope's most famous photographs was taken over a few months of an apparently empty portion of space, about the tenth of the size of a full moon. This Ultra Deep Field photograph turned out to contain about ten thousand galaxies. Or viewing a photograph of our closest galactic neighbor, Andromeda, may strike us that this galaxy is so far away that its light has taken 2.5 million years to reach us; that we are looking at this galaxy as it existed before *Homo sapiens* roamed the earth. Reflecting on the immense size of this galaxy and its distance from us may shrivel our existence before the vastness of space and time, where categories may dissolve and no longer appear clear and helpful, where certainties evaporate, and where we find ourselves again in a position for growth and for reconsidering our lives.

Our self-knowledge is suspect. The psalmist asks, "Who can detect their errors?" (Ps 19:12). What we think we know about ourselves is sometimes warped or wrong. We are now keenly aware of how distorted and self-serving our memories are. Our memories are not the fastidious librarian dutifully cataloging every event in our lives for perfect retrieval in the future. If our memories are a library, well, someone has plundered the shelves, ripped up various books, altered others, hidden a bunch, and added some, too. The blind spots in our eyes are invisible to us. We conveniently fill in the void of our vision. Nor can we see the derisive look on our face, but this is what we need to see. Thus, self-analysis alone is insufficient for living a good life. Self-examination is often self-serving. We hate living with cognitive dissonance, so we quickly justify or dismiss our faults, and our memories are co-conspirators—far more malleable than the time and space we inhabit.

> No man ever understands quite his own artful dodges to escape from the grim shadow of self-knowledge.
>
> —JOSEPH CONRAD, *LORD JIM*[17]

We suffer from confirmation bias. We accept evidence that confirms our existing beliefs and disregard contrary evidence. As Judge Taylor says in *To Kill A Mockingbird*, "People generally see what they look for, and hear what they listen for."[18] We believe what we want to believe. We see what we expect to see. Psychologist Cordelia Fine in *A Mind of Its Own: How Your Brain Distorts and Deceives* notes the disheartening fact that in light of contrary evidence we are *more* likely to cling to our beliefs. How can that be? When faced with contrary evidence, our brain quickly dismisses it, and then we exclaim, "Well, if *that's* the best that the other side can come up with then I really must be right."[19] Fine writes, "Once acquired, even the most erroneous beliefs enjoy an undeserved degree of protection from rejection and revision."[20] According to Fine, our brains have sophisticated mechanisms for protecting our ego, warping reality, and convincing us that we are right. There is now a mountain of evidence to show that "the brain evades, twists, discounts, misinterprets, even makes up evidence—all so that we can retain that satisfying sense of being in the right."[21]

Once, while perusing news sites, I saw an article heading: "Why dogs are smarter than cats." As a cat lover and "owner" of three gorgeous cats, I dismissed it with a shrug. The arguments would have been flimsy, and I would have emerged even more convinced that cats are superior. Of course cats are smarter—how else can I explain my suspicion that my cats are Zen masters who have apparently figured out the life worth living? Later, I came across an article: "Cat people are smarter than dog people," which I read. Enlightening piece!

In the classic film *The Gods Must Be Crazy*, a bushman traps a baboon using a simple trick. Place some nuts inside an immovable object that has a narrow opening—wide enough for a baboon to slide a hand through, but too narrow to pull out its hand if it grabs the nuts, because it has made a fist. As expected, the baboon puts in its hand, grabs the food, but now can't escape because it won't let go.[22] Like this baboon, we sometimes have difficulty reasoning ourselves out of situations and opening ourselves to different options and opinions. "I have the nuts, and no one is going to convince me that this isn't a brilliant solution."

Once we get an idea in our heads, it is notoriously difficult to eradicate. We seek to confirm our beliefs, ideas, and views. So, when people tell us we are intelligent, or beautiful, or witty, we happily believe them. (Psychopaths and narcissists take advantage of this trait by using their charm to manipulate people.) If we fail, well, it is some other person's fault or some other cause of events. If we succeed, it is because of our insightful brilliance and competence. We live in Lake Wobegon[23] where we all think we are above average. We are more intelligent than most, funnier, and harder working. Our failures are minimal or the result of other people's faults, but our successes are because of our great charm, ability, and perspicacity. We are the norm—everyone else is abnormal or extreme. Thus George Carlin joked, "Anyone who is driving slower than you is an idiot, and anyone driving faster than you is a maniac."[24]

We assume that if we give the correct explanation, a good argument, or some substantial evidence, then people will give up their erroneous views. But we forget that our beliefs and opinions have utility. They are beneficial to us, they justify our lives and behavior, they confirm our views of the world, and they keep us tied to our communities. It is thus understandable why Thomas Paine said, "Time makes more converts than reason." There is often a prohibitive cost involved in giving up our beliefs and views.

This also presents a problem for writers. Should writers shun explanations and arguments because readers will believe whatever they want? Or should we target a specific audience most likely to agree with us? Or should we write in impenetrable language so that, apart from people valuing something the more effort they put into it, the obscure language is fertile ground for ambiguity? Write in highfalutin language, let readers simply apply the interpretation that fits their prevailing views (that they will not change anyway), and they will think the writer is quite brilliant because the book confirmed what they were already thinking.

Even if we intellectually acknowledge that our brains are great distorters and deceivers, this knowledge is exceptionally difficult to apply to ourselves. In addition, we are lazy—it takes a significant amount of mental and emotional energy to change deeply-held views. It takes effort to think, but far more effort to change one's mind. Thus, some fall for fake news and any rubbish people say. We seek cognitive shortcuts, while inundated with over a hundred cognitive biases.[25] Here is where disruption is useful. We need to be outmaneuvered. Our perceived strengths, which overshadow our failings, need to be rendered irrelevant. Our defenses and strongholds need shaking.

The value of disruption is that it reveals areas for change, and change is an essential ingredient for a life worth living. We need a prod, a push, and sometimes a jolt. Disruption is like a flash of lightning during a storm that for a moment illuminates the surrounding darkness, and, depending on how close it is, can raise our hair or shock and shake us into heightened awareness of our surrounding reality. Disruption is useful because it brings to the forefront of consciousness our predicament.

Victor Hugo's *Les Misérables* was once required reading for many church ministers—an understandable requirement given Hugo's unforgettable characters and themes of adversity, poverty, slavery, the abuse of legal systems, death, compassion, forgiveness, and redemption. At the beginning of the novel, Jean Valjean, who has spent nineteen years in jail (which has turned him into a hardened man), is released and finds himself welcomed into the house of an old bishop, Monseigneur Myriel. Myriel leads a frugal life and has given away his wealth except for two valuables: silver plates and candlesticks. During the night, Valjean returns the bishop's kindness by stealing his silver plates and hightailing it out the door. As happened before, the law catches up with Valjean and the police want to know how such a wretched man has come into possession of valuable silver. "Ah, you say the bishop gave it to you—well, let's find out." The police drag Valjean back to Myriel's house. To Valjean's incomprehension, Myriel says, "I gave these to him, and he forgot to take the candlesticks." This remarkable act of love is the disruptive moment that catalyzes the transformation of Valjean into an honest and gracious man. Jean Valjean lives a long, good, and worthwhile life, and his kindness cascades down the generations. Valjean's death at the end of the novel comes as he bequeaths these candlesticks to his daughter Cosette, and he dies with the light from the candlesticks falling on his face. The candlesticks—signs of remarkable disruptive love—make fitting bookends to the novel.

When does change begin? In answering this question, different fields of inquiry inevitably fall back to a disruptive influence: whether it is a novelist describing the transformation of a character in a story—an inciting action that is the start of the grand adventure—or a theologian speaking of character formed through the darkness of suffering, or a developmental psychologist speaking of "disequilibrium"—a conflict that is an essential part of growth—or a biologist speaking of evolution as an introduction of a dislocation into an underlying continuity, or a physicist speaking of creativity occurring at the edge of chaos. When life is too stable, nothing changes. When life is too disorderly, destruction results. But on the edge is where we find newness and creativity. In chaos theory, it is on the boundary where there is enough disorganization to allow for old structures to be undone and new ones to be formed, which incidentally brings us full circle from science back to religion. Several ancient creation myths, including the biblical narrative, have chaos as an important theme. New creation and chaos are surprisingly interconnected.

When we ask someone about when change has occurred in their life, people will invariably answer that it began with some form of disruption. They will mention *lupus in fabula*—the wolf in the story—the disruptive element in the tale of their lives. Disruption is the catalyst. Scientists seek to discover the nature of particles by smashing them together, or try to understand the nature of materials by placing them under extreme pressure. Likewise, we hardly know ourselves until we are tested. Self-scrutiny has limited value. We need a disruptive situation to scrutinize us. If there is some darkness in the heart, we will discover it on the disruptive journey.

Transforming our relationships often begins with disruption. When our lives are stable, we comfortably accept feedback that reinforces our prevailing views and identity. We believe our intentions, motives, and actions are good and honorable—that we are doing things for the right reasons, for the greater good, for the benefit of others. Being open to pursuing a good life, however, is being receptive to disruptive feedback that we allow to continue to loop back and reorganize our thinking and ways of living. For remarkable change to occur, this disruption needn't be a terrible hardship; it may be as small as a brief insightful conversation—a flapping of a butterfly's wing—that amplifies through our entire life, eventually forming a hurricane that sweeps away old views, categories of thought, and ways of relating. And if chaos theory is anything to go by, change can occur remarkably quickly.

Relationships disrupt

Disruption will arrive unannounced at our doorstep and sometimes barge in without knocking. Dislocation will arrive from our relationships, often through friends, relatives, partners, spouses, and kids.

Unfortunately, we often listen the least to those who know us the best. But if disruption is the beginning of change, the next time we feel a twang of discomfort when a friend or partner asks us a question or makes a comment, we can pause to consider.

We can go further. To improve our relationships, we can make disruption intentional. We can ask our closest friends or relatives what they wish we would change. For example, couples sometimes find that therapy has been beneficial for their marriage. One reason is that it intensifies disruption by providing an opportunity to listen more intently to one's partner and an opportunity for a psychologist to question ways of relating—which incidentally is why therapists prefer a good question rather than an excellent answer. An answer may enlighten, but a good question—now that can be disruptive.

A marriage or partnership can be a powerful impetus for growth; likewise with raising children. Often disruption isn't even on the horizon when parents consider raising their kids. For example, many books or seminars on parenting that give advice on how to raise children implicitly operate with the view that parents "have it all together," and now here is a book or a program to help "sort out your kids." Many Christians adopt an approach that is based on their Scriptures, such as the proverb: "folly is bound up in the heart of a child" (Prov 22:15), and thus it is their job to straighten out their kids. You may labor in vain to find any chapters in parenting books such as "You're more muddled than your kids," "How you can make less noise around the house," or "The ten ways you exasperate your children." By skipping the disruptive element, such books and seminars miss the foundation for relational growth. After all, if folly is bound up in the heart of a child (presumably because they're our kids), how much folly is bound up in the heart of a parent? Take lying as one example. We can easily catch children in lies. But adults? Many studies show that as we grow up, we become better at lying; until between ages eighteen to twenty-four, it is almost impossible to tell accurately whether someone is lying. Despite the popular assumption that we can tell if an adult is lying—whether through lack of eye contact, tics, body movement, sweating, or voice—studies find we are about 47 percent accurate.[26] No one grows a Pinocchio's nose when they lie. In other words, if we are trying to figure out whether an adult is lying, we have slightly worse odds than if we flipped a coin. And when we think about it, the best liars couldn't care less about feeling guilty or ashamed, so why would they sweat about it?

Disruption also visits larger communities and nations. Wars, economic collapse, pandemics, or an environmental disaster can disruptively reveal the indifference, greed, or crimes of nations. Such events can show where nations undermine the quest for the life worth living. A community or nation opens itself to transformation when it allows disruption to provide an opportunity to consider its behavior as an entire group. National reflection, such as the work of the South African Truth and Reconciliation Commission, provides an occasion for national disruption, repentance, and forgiveness. It is good when people in the United States reflect on the nation's sobering and inexorable destruction of Native Americans, its role in nineteenth-century slavery, or its use of atomic weapons. The growing realization that the use of atomic weapons were war crimes can help towards the eradication of these weapons of mass destruction.[27] Compared to Germany, Japan has struggled to come to terms with its World War II atrocities; for instance, the Second Sino-Japanese War and the sexual slavery of Koreans. This doesn't bode well for healthy relations with these geographic neighbors. Or consider the child abuse scandal that hit the church—one of the worst evils to tarnish the institution—a disruptive tsunami that contains the possibility for remarkable community transformation. But with any form of disruption, there is also the opportunity for cover-up, minimizing, stonewalling, blaming, and hardening.

Another example that has implications for transformation in Christianity is the need for disruption of theological categories. Entrenched theological views within Christianity are often a significant hindrance to the life worth living. Take some uncontroversial points today: the views that heretics should be exiled, tortured, or killed; Jews get what they deserve for killing Jesus; blacks should serve whites; women are inferior—all were once ingrained theological positions that caused vast atrocities and untold relational harm.

For our relationships to thrive, we need to know that we can be wrong. Unfortunately, many Christian theological expressions are geared toward the exact opposite. And once you think you have arrived at the summit of truth, it's a quick step before you start violently imposing it on everyone else. This runs like: We have the message of the gospel figured out. Our approach to interpreting the Bible is correct. Our tradition is the best. Our view of Jesus is correct. Our theological system is the pinnacle to which all others should aspire. But this is grasping the wind. I once owned a series of books published by Zondervan on different evangelical theological views, ten titles in all, but there are now thirty-eight books in the Counterpoints series. The titles read:

- Two views on women in ministry
- Five views on sanctification
- Three views on creation and evolution
- Five views on apologetics
- Five views on law and gospel
- Are miraculous gifts for today? Four views
- Four views on hell
- Three views on the millennium and beyond
- Three views on the rapture
- Four views on salvation in a pluralistic world

Just from these titles, that is 432,000 possible theological combinations. Even evangelicals, who pride themselves in being right, in attempting to identify the "correct" theological truth, have a constellation of hundreds of thousands to choose from. And this is just considering ten books from only one section of Christianity. You have a better chance over your lifespan of being struck by lightning (about one in ten thousand) than figuring out the "right" theological view. This is chasing the wind, because even if you somehow figured out the "correct" view, it won't stay correct for long. The knowledge and information we have today will soon be outdated and there are scientific studies to show that this happens in predictable ways.

Knowledge has a decay rate, as explained well in Samuel Arbesman's *The Half-Life of Facts: Why Everything We Know Has an Expiration Date*.[28] According to Arbesman, knowledge is like a radioactive isotope. We cannot predict when a single atom of uranium will decay, but we can predict what will happen to a large body of uranium. Uranium 235 has a half-life of 708.3 million years, so if we start with a chunk of U_{235}, in 708.3 million years it will only contain half that initial amount of uranium. Likewise, with knowledge, we cannot tell when a particular fact will evaporate into the netherworld, but a body of knowledge will decay. Arbesman summarizes the research that shows this change happens in predictable ways. For example, in the medical field, by analyzing about five hundred journal articles on cirrhosis and hepatitis and discovering what material is now disproven, out of date, or still factual, researchers find that this knowledge has a half-life of about forty-five years.[29] Other fields have shorter half-lives, for example, computer science or nuclear physics. Even if you happen, by some miracle, to stumble upon the "correct" body of knowledge, in a few decades a substantial portion of your knowledge will be out of date. Thus, there are good reasons scholars are more skeptical of sources cited that are more than a few decades old.

If we so neatly categorize our thinking and place inviolable frameworks on our understanding, we are increasingly subject both to cognitive dissonance and confirmation bias, and then there is little room for growth and transformation. We then become intolerant of any disruption to our carefully crafted thought categories, and if someone proposes a novel way to look at things, then watch the fur fly.

Categories of thinking—philosophical, scientific, medical, religious, ethical, political—all change. And we change. There was a time, growing up in apartheid South Africa, when I thought Nelson Mandela was a terrorist and Desmond Tutu was undermining Christianity. I once argued with Tutu, as an undergraduate student in South Africa, over a theological point about how salvation was more important than freedom for blacks, and that everyone should submit to the government (Rom 13), which incidentally is illustrative that one can make the Bible serve any purpose. Many South African churches supported the status quo of apartheid and agreed that to campaign for blacks to get the vote was to confuse the gospel message with politics. But more than that, I felt superior to black people. Shameful as this is to recount today, it was normal. I was part of a white community that was generally united by opposing the likes of Mandela and Tutu. I went to an all-white private boarding school, which was like Hogwarts but without the fun or magic. No blacks were allowed in our schools, in our neighborhoods, on our beaches, in our bathrooms, or on our public transport. They could come into our houses—if they were servants. Today, Mandela and Tutu are rightly admired and remembered for their courage, kindness, and moral insight.

We underestimate how much we will change over our lifetime. Psychologists call this "the end of history illusion."[30] We know we are not the same people we were ten years ago, but we consistently underestimate how much we will change in the next decade. Our future selves may very well laugh or cringe at our present selves.

When God shows up

In keeping with our dialog with Christianity, we should now note that disruption is in fact a neglected but central theme in Christian stories. The Bible is not a paragon of virtuous characters. And who in the Bible highlights their relational failure? In Christian stories, God arrives and outmaneuvers people, either directly, or by using other people, or by using the circumstances of life. When God shows up, God disrupts. We see this clearly in the stories about Jesus.

Jesus routinely unsettles people. He allows unclean people to touch him. He eats with sinners and drunkards—so much so that the community leaders label him a "sinner." The New Testament describes him as a different messiah from what many people expected. He is peaceful toward the Romans. He socializes with people whom "civil" society has dismissed. And the stories Jesus tells turn life and limb upside down. The last are first, and the first are last. Those that we would expect to be the heroes turn out to be the villains, and vice versa. The stories of Jesus' birth, life, death, and resurrection are all told with a disruptive quality.

Consider how Jesus outmaneuvers a rich man who runs up to Jesus and asks what he must do to inherit eternal life (Mark 10:17–22). Jesus' answer is that he must keep the commandments, such as not stealing, lying, committing adultery, or murder. What is the rich man's reply? "Teacher,

I have kept all these since my youth." Here we have an upright citizen, a person who observes the Jewish law. We may say that this man's position of strength is his moral certainty—that he has kept all these commandments since his youth. Note that Jesus does not debate him on his perceived position of strength. Rather, Jesus looks at him and says, "You lack one thing; go, sell what you own, and give the money to the poor, and you will have treasure in heaven; then come, follow me" (Mark 10:21).

Ah yes, there is one other minor detail we left out—money! And this detail has the propensity to expose many crazy behaviors and overwhelming desires for power, security, reputation, or comfort. Like Honore de Balzac's disruptive observation, "Behind every great fortune lies a great crime," which raises the important questions regarding wealth: How did you gain it? And why you are keeping it?

Jesus addresses the one area that exposes the rich man, disrupts him, and renders his "strength" irrelevant. There is no more talk about how he has kept the commandments. The rich man is now in a place where he can see himself more clearly. The story ends with possibility. We read that the rich man went away "shocked" and "distressed." We may say *disrupted*.

Jesus' parables have a Nathanic[31] twist to them. The stories came with disruptive force to their hearers and leave the readers of these parables with questions:

Are we those who have been forgiven, yet we throttle people for what they owe us? (Parable of the Unmerciful Servant: Matt 18:21–35).

Are we the priest or Levite who pass by on the other side of the road, often ignoring those in need, while those whom we despise out-love us? (Parable of the Good Samaritan: Luke 10:25–37).

When God shows up, God disrupts, and often with a question:

- To Adam and Eve in the garden, "Where are you?"
- To Cain, "Where is your brother?"
- To Jonah outside Nineveh, "Is it right for you to be angry?"
- To Job, "Where were you when I laid the foundation of the earth?"

Much of the disruption in the biblical stories is an upheaval of theological categories—the way people understood God, and what they believed God required. This disruption went beyond the Pharisees and teachers of the law to major figures in the Bible. Abraham, Job, Peter, Paul—all had their theological views disrupted, undermined, or rendered irrelevant. Peter can hardly take one step without some disturbance to his theology, whether it is by Jesus, or by Paul (Gal 2), or by a vision from heaven (Acts 10:11–16).

In the Christian story, God subverts expectations. This story is often called "apocalyptic," a word that carries the idea of a disruption, a revelation, an unveiling, a breaking in of the future—a future that dislocates and overturns categories of the present and the past. This disruption brings something new, something different, and something better from what has gone before.

The easiest person to fool

Nobel laureate and physicist Richard Feynman loved to say, "The first principle is that you must not fool yourself—and you are the easiest person to fool."[32] But that can't be right. Someone else is the fool, not me. Thus, we outwardly condemn our hidden desires, fit our own cognitive blinders, construct our memories, and hide our secrets from ourselves.

The Devil's Dictionary by Ambrose Bierce provides this amusing definition for "Saint" and supplies an accompanying anecdote:

> **Saint**, n. A dead sinner revised and edited.
>
> The Duchess of Orleans relates that the irreverent old calumniator, Marshal Villeroi, who in his youth had known St. Francis de Sales, said, on hearing him called saint: "I am delighted to hear that Monsieur de Sales is a saint. He was fond of saying indelicate things, and used to cheat at cards. In other respects he was a perfect gentleman, though a fool."[33]

If the Marshal's recollection was correct, it would be just another addition to the long list of those who outwardly condemn that to which they are secretly attached. Saint Francis de Sales (1567–1622), Bishop of Geneva, is famous for his *Introduction to the Devout Life*, where under the section *Prohibited Games*, he writes, "Games of dice, cards, and the like in which winning depends principally on chance are not only dangerous as recreations, just as dancing is, but are of their own simple nature bad and reprehensible. This is why they have been forbidden both by civil and ecclesiastical law."[34]

Why condemn that which we secretly love? Such tactics bamboozle us and deflect attention. Surely others can't possibly think that we would be guilty of what we condemn. It is a truism that those who condemn others are often covertly attached to the things they condemn. Projection is commonplace and a tactic for fooling ourselves. Hence another reason disruption is valuable, but we may not always welcome it.

What is our response to disruption? Sometimes we resist it. Even though we are outmaneuvered, we fight back, flailing our arms, and mumbling how life is unfair, how people misunderstand us, and if other people hadn't messed up so badly, things would be different. Faced with dislocation, we resist with an arsenal of tactics. We get angry and cut the other person off; we mope around and isolate ourselves; we gossip and focus on someone else's problem; we distract and play people off against each other; we give some brilliant excuse or a shrug of dismissal.

The path of self-justification is always available and enticing. An alternative theory is forever within grasp. We only have to recall a court trial to remind ourselves that we can always place a unique spin on the evidence—even if the evidence is obvious to everyone else. An excuse is always available for our behavior. There is always someone or something to blame. For every plain and rational explanation, there is a conspiracy theory. In the path of an avalanche of evidence, we still find people clinging to the most tenuous of ideas and possibilities.

In the movie-musical *Chicago*, Richard Gere, playing the part of a high-price lawyer Billy Flynn, recounts a scene where a woman named Kitty discovers her partner Harry in bed with two other women. Startled, Harry blurts out, "What? I'm alone . . . are you going to believe what you see or what I tell you?" She shoots him.[35]

What's the poor guy to say? If he had some training in Christian apologetics, he may have protested:

"Hang on dear, your presuppositions are causing you to misinterpret the facts and have distorted your perception of the truth."

"You don't believe in God, so you don't have an objective moral standard by which to judge me!"

"It's logically possible that these women just appeared in my bed while I was sleeping and without my knowledge."

But none of this helps or changes reality—like a disorientated pilot in a fog, refusing to rely on his instruments and instead trusting his disorientated senses, flies into the ground. The reality outside the cockpit trumps false assumptions, beliefs, and impressions. Here is a case where instincts and feelings are jarringly disconnected from reality. Your inner ear is saying that you are flying level, but your instruments show you are in a dive, your airspeed is in the red, and you have seconds to pull up. Your instruments display reality, and your mind must reason itself out. Pilots need to condition their brains to accept what their instruments are telling them, and this is difficult to do. VFR (visual flight rules) into IMC (instrument meteorological conditions) is avoidable and the primary cause of accidents in general aviation, from JFK Jr. to Kobe Bryant. We all have presuppositions, assumptions, beliefs, and feelings that we need to question and adjust, using the best tools and instruments available to us.

Welcoming disruption involves a new view of ourselves—one where we are not as smart, upright, kind, or as patient as we think. Disruption provides an opportunity to see the relational damage we inflict. It grabs our perceived strengths and excellent qualities and renders them irrelevant. It outmaneuvers us and exposes the junk in our lives that we hide away. It takes what we excel at, the areas we have in control, the parts we have sorted out, and snatches them all away and leaves us in a position to change.

One thing is certain: disruption will arrive whether we welcome it or not. Even given the benefits of disruption, it can only take us so far in the quest for the good life. Disruption by itself brings minor change. The disruptive flash of lightning not only awakens us, it also briefly illuminates the roads we have traveled and the roads we may take. Disruption brings us to a place where we can recognize our need for change and embrace it, or where we can resist and reject it.

Chapter 2

Welcome to the Real World: An Examined Life

> "I have done that," says my memory. "I cannot have done that," says my pride, and remains inexorable. Eventually—memory yields.
>
> —Nietzsche

> The true voyage of discovery consists not of going to new places, but of having a new pair of eyes.
>
> —Proust

> The hardest victory is the victory over self.
>
> —Aristotle

An examined life

Given our propensity for self-protection and excuses, even if we have the desire to understand ourselves, the obstacles to the examined life are considerable. The ancient appeal above the temple of Apollo at Delphi to "know yourself" is far harder than it first sounds. None of us have a panoptic view of ourselves. The way we think our voice sounds differs from how others hear it, so a recording of our voice sounds strange to us. Even the key feature by which we relate to other people—our face—is hidden from us.

When we see our face, it is as a reflection, which is usually not the reality we are looking for—all serene and calm (like the eye of a hurricane?). In addition, our reflection is a laterally inverted image, so even here we are seeing a version of ourselves that doesn't exist.

Of course, we can also see our face in a photograph, but these are also distorted pictures of reality. Many of us have seen a photo of ourselves grinning like the Cheshire cat, but recall being annoyed at the time. The social media post of a happy family on holiday may conceal the fight the kids just had, the snarky comments between a couple, the stress of travel, or even the argument to take everyone's picture and smile. We are selective about what we portray and remember. A picture is worth a thousand words . . . of set-ups and cover-ups . . . especially with Photoshop. The "Gorilla Experiment"[36] showed many of us just how selective our brain is and how easily anything deemed non-relevant by our brain is hidden from our consciousness.

Reality is hard, and hard to accept. Do we want to know the reality of our lives? Can we? In Jane Wagner's Broadway show, the comedian Lily Tomlin quipped, "Reality is the leading cause of stress amongst those in touch with it."[37] There is a clinical term for this: *depressive realism*—those who are depressed but have an accurate view of themselves and their situation. Humor can shield us from the harsh realities of life, and to our advantage, we all live with a measure of denial. Too much reality is overwhelming, but small doses are essential for the good life. Some reality about our lives and relationships are worth the pain of exposure.

An iconic movie representation of this idea was the Matrix trilogy by the Wachowski siblings. In the first film of the *Matrix* trilogy, the main character, Neo, in an event of considerable disruption, wakes up to find that his whole life is a dream—that what he thought was real is a virtual world created by machines that have enslaved humanity. These machines, who have taken over the world, have plugged humans into a matrix, a computer simulation, to keep them enslaved.[38]

The film raises the question: What if we woke up to find the reality about ourselves to be worse than we thought? And once tasting this reality, would we want to go back to our prior ignorance? Neo asks after he is free from the Matrix and his life as a slave to machines:

"I can't go back, can I?"

Morpheus replies, "No, but if you could, would you?"

Another character named Cypher feels differently. He loathes his newfound reality and ends up betraying his small group of survivors. In reward for his betrayal, Cypher finagles a deal with the machines to put him back inside the simulation. For Cypher, it is far better to be in a computer simulation feasting on a nice juicy steak than to be living in the real world eating dregs.

Philosophy and Christianity have connected an examined life to a worthwhile life. The gadfly Socrates, who delighted in asking the disruptive question to undermine a point of view, gave a memorable maxim at his trial: "An unexamined life is not worth living."[39] What makes a life good? Is the good life always pleasurable and happy? Is the good life one where you are healthy, wealthy, and wise, but in a computer simulation? Why not get a *Total Recall*-style implant that inserts fake memories of a grand life and provides the right electrical and chemical stimulus to make you think that your life is good? Why refuse to live in a world where your brain is manipulated to think that you have a life where you are wealthy, famous, and powerful, where you are even renowned for your generosity and love? Is that the good life? Why would we reject a life so "lived"? Is there a difference between life and an illusion of life? These questions will remain as people more fully immerse themselves in virtual worlds.

Our conceptual frameworks and beliefs have changed, and for the better. Over time, our views on gods, slavery, distinct races, women, rights for children and animals, the LGBTQ community, and our environment have all changed. The earth has been decentralized, and we now find our humanity connected to other species through the evolutionary process. Views of matter, energy, time, and space are vastly different today than they were prior to the twentieth century. Awakening to reality is a constant and continuing process, so we should expect radical changes to our understanding in the future.

Are there ways that we can further encourage this awakening to the reality of our lives, and what exactly are we looking for?

Nowadays, when we want to find out something, we may search the omniscient and omnipresent Google. Or if our computer is acting weird, we run a virus scan. Is it possible to run an analogous virus scan of our lives and figure out what is wrong? Can we Google ourselves, and through introspection search ourselves and retrieve the information we need? What would we find if we mentally searched and tried to inventory our faults and foibles? This is not as scary or as productive as it might first sound. With this type of self-examination:

- We end up with only a pile of information, which is usually not the insight we need.
- The information is filtered. Our memory has paid advertising money to have some results displayed first.

- The mass of information may well overwhelm the essential piece that we need. Perhaps the relevant information is on hit number 16,356,952.
- Just as Google filters our search results based on our previous web habits and locations, so our confirmation bias tailors the search results.

We can rummage through a massive filing cabinet of information, but perhaps the answer we need is in the next room. Are there better metaphors than Google or virus scans for seeing the reality of our lives and relationships? Are there more effective methods than looking at ourselves in the mirror and hoping for illumination?

Aleksandr Solzhenitsyn, in his *Gulag Archipelago*, recalls a moment after the state security forces arrested him and he considered the nasty people who had arrested him. He asked himself: How much different am I from my captor? If I were in their shoes, and if my life had turned out differently, would I be capable of doing these things? It is in this context that we find his often-quoted statement that "the line between good and evil cuts through the heart of every human being."[40]

Solzhenitsyn illustrates a more productive avenue to follow—a path that looks to others for self-examination. The better mirror is closer than the one in our bathroom; it is the person sitting next to us. Often, the clearest way to see ourselves is in the face of others. The person in the best position to tell us what we are like is the one beside us—the person to whom we relate. After all, they are on the receiving end. They see our face or see the way we turn our face away; they hear our words and feel their weight. We build relational health by being receptive to the input of others and recognizing that, regarding our failures, other people often know us better than we know ourselves.

There are two ways people can be a mirror.

First, they experience our words, looks, and behavior. They feel the full weight of our words, and if we give them a chance, they will echo back to us the reality of our lives. Mirror-like, they reflect their experience of us. Through their eyes we see our reflection. Learning that other people are the best mirrors encourages us to invite feedback and is a crucial step in the examined life. The next time someone addresses our behavior, instead of responding with silence or with the snap "What's your problem?!," we can ask "Why do you say that?"

Second, we all share the same humanity, and therefore we can see ourselves in others. We often hear of six degrees of separation between people—that we are connected to everyone else on the planet through at most six people. With recent experiments and our increasing technological interconnectedness, we are down to about four degrees of separation today.

But what about a psychological test to see how close we are to the person we have contempt for, the scandalous, the materialistic, those who exalt themselves, the racist, the sexist, the self-righteous. Is it four degrees? Two? One? Psychological experiments show that under certain circumstances, we have similarities with those whom we despise.[41] Humankind's ability to be cruel, vain, and greedy is not limited to those making the national headlines. What do we have in common with other people, including the people we dislike? It is easy to create categories and explanations for why the people we dislike are so different from us. What is hard to discover are the similarities.

According to the Hebrew Bible, the prophet Nathan once came before King David and recounted to him a painful story about two men—one poor, the other rich. The poor man's only possession was a beloved pet lamb. The rich man who had many sheep, however, stole this poor man's lamb and slaughtered it for a feast. In 2 Samuel 12:5, we read that David burns with anger against the rich man and says to Nathan, "As the Lord lives, the man who has done this deserves to die . . . because he had no pity." David's response is "right" in the sense that the rich man had committed a terrible crime, but David is wrong in the application. David's first instinct is not "How am I like this rich man?" which, as we know, was Nathan's point. David was this rich man because he had killed Uriah the Hittite and abducted Uriah's wife. It bears repeating that sometimes the characteristics that we denounce in others are like those found in us. Sometimes we openly despise behaviors that resemble our conduct that we are ashamed of. When, however, we use other people as mirrors of our own lives, their weaknesses and failures serve as a reflection of our own.

We should make one concession. Jean-Paul Sartre in his play *No Exit* tells the story of two women and a man who are in hell and are locked in a room together.[42] The one woman has lived her life in light of men's desire, and she wants a mirror. The other woman says that she will be a mirror, but she has her own prejudices. Sartre describes a scene wherein hell is other people—where another person is reflecting their own manipulative vision. So, the mirror of others can be distorted and flat-out wrong. These scheming tactics are how people maintain power and control and keep others in abusive or codependent relationships. Consider the source. Yes, sometimes we need to let people keep their crazy, manipulative views to themselves. But often the mirror is all too clear and spot-on, and the right people can become more than a mirror, a goal to which we can aspire.

Jesus tells his disciples that before they try to take the speck out of someone else's eye they must first take out the plank in their own eye (Luke 6:41). But wait a minute. If we are all messed up, how come I have the plank and she only has a speck? The reason is that we have strong tendencies to think too highly of ourselves.

The opening lines of *The Great Gatsby* reads: "In my younger and more vulnerable years my father gave me some advice that I've been turning over in my mind ever since. 'Whenever you feel like criticizing any one,' he told me, 'just remember that all the people in this world haven't had the advantages that you've had.'"[43] Apart from the good advice to imagine yourself in another's place, these words imply that self-reflection isn't something easily achieved: "I have been turning over in my mind ever since." The examined life is an ongoing process of imagination, and a failure of relational growth is often a failure of imagination. A lack of imagination hinders our ability to put ourselves in the place of another. Our imagination can teleport us into a different, albeit fantasy or hypothetical circumstance, and allow us to question ourselves. What would we be like if we had similar temptations, disadvantages, upbringing, stresses, opportunities, relationships, and environment? Can we see how their faults could have been ours? And from this type of self-examination blossoms two vital characteristics—humility and compassion. It is for reasons such as these that an examined life is necessary for a life well lived.

How to be right and look good

There is one pervasive and significant human propensity that undermines the examined life, and it deserves a separate section: self-justification.

Yogi Berra once said, "I really didn't say everything I said."[44] How easily we dissect with scalpel-like precision what we said—to explain away our words and to clarify what we would have liked to have meant. Even with disruption throwing us off balance and feedback from others providing evidence of our failures, we still leap to wild theories, projection, splitting, complaining, minimizing, and blaming—all to clench a meticulously crafted view of ourselves. The mind's incredible capability for self-justification erects roadblocks on the highway to the worthwhile life—blocked off with ten patrol cars, lights flashing, sirens blaring, and ready to stop any further progress.

Our memories and mental gymnastics are remarkable when arguing. Scrutinizing the other person, we are the sharpest tool in the toolbox, capable of exposing the slightest frown we saw, parsing the smallest lilt in the voice, and sniffing out any hint of deviation from the "facts." But when faced with something foolish or nasty we did, we speedily say, "I don't remember it that way," or "You took what I said out of context." Like most lawyers, we are more interested in winning and uncovering the truth only if it helps our case.

Of course, sometimes it is right to defend ourselves, but these are less frequent than we think. And why the frantic, intense rush to defend ourselves? Why do we interrupt and cut others short to explain ourselves? Often, our explanations are ridiculous to everyone except ourselves, like the captain of the capsized cruise ship Costa Concordia when explaining why he left the sinking ship before everyone else: "I fell into the lifeboat."[45]

Even when we decide to give a genuine apology, our commitment can evaporate into the netherworld once we start talking. In one of my favorite scenes in the British TV sitcom *Fawlty Towers*, Basil Fawlty, the owner of a hotel, has just ordered a bunch of guests to vacate the premises—all because Basil mistakenly believes that these guests were engaging in non-marital sex. But then his wife corrects him and assures him that nothing untoward has been going on; but now he must apologize to the guests. At first Basil resists, yelling, "Is this what made Britain great—I'm so sorry I made a mistake?!" He then concedes and runs upstairs to the guests' room, repeating to himself "I'm so sorry I made a mistake . . . I'm so sorry I made a mistake . . ." He bursts through the door, exclaiming, "I'm so sorry but my *wife* has made a dreadful mistake."[46]

Social psychologists Carol Tavris and Elliot Aronson in *Mistakes Were Made (but Not By Me): Why We Justify Foolish Beliefs, Bad Decisions, and Hurtful Acts* draw from a multitude of experiments and research to paint a sobering picture that because of cognitive dissonance that drives self-justification, "most of us find it difficult, if not impossible, to say, "I was wrong: I made a terrible mistake."[47] Their many and diverse examples make for enlightening and sober reading—all those *other* people who can't see their mistakes, who refused to admit they were wrong when faced with overwhelming evidence, and who blamed someone else. From politicians such as Henry Kissinger, who, when confronted with accusations of his horrendous war crimes in South East Asia and South America, offered this glib remark: "Mistakes were quite possibly made by the administration in which I served,"[48] to George W. Bush who refused to admit he was wrong—about WMDs in Iraq, that Saddam was in cahoots with Al-Qaeda, and that the conflict would be over quickly—justifying a war that killed over a hundred thousand people, caused countless life-altering injuries and post-traumatic stress disorders, and cost over one trillion dollars.[49] Other examples include psychologists who were part of the disastrous recovered-memory therapy movement, to doctors who made medical mistakes, to prosecutors who secured convictions for people later exonerated. Very few apologize.

Tavris and Aronson ask, "How in the world can they *live* with themselves? The answer is: exactly the way the rest of us do."[50]

Peter Malkin, a member of the Mossad team that captured Adolf Eichmann in Argentina in 1960, authored a book called *Eichmann in My Hands*[51] describing his experience and conversations with Eichmann. For Malkin, the most shocking part of the Eichmann story was Eichmann's extraordinary capacity for self-justification. Journalists and other observers at Eichmann's subsequent trial in Jerusalem likewise half expected to find themselves confronted by an inhuman monster. But sitting there was a man who seemed to look and behave like any other old man.

This mundane bureaucrat led to Hannah Arendt's controversial yet memorable phrase "the banality of evil."[52] On the one hand, there is a shallowness and ordinariness to evil, the familiarity of an old person, a commonality to our shared humanity. In Arendt's words, evil is in fact "thought defying," because it is so shallow and without any depth that thought can penetrate. On the other hand, Eichmann—the adept administrator of the Holocaust who kept all the trains running and reported directly to Himmler—was a mass murderer who knew what he was doing. Eichmann said at the end of the war in his farewell speech to subordinates, "I will laugh when I leap into the grave because I have the feeling that I have killed five million Jews. That gives me great satisfaction and gratification." That is evil, but not banal.

Self-justification is the reason even war criminals and torturers appear quite content to live with themselves. Self-justification uses

- blame—our victims simply got what they deserve;
- dehumanization—these people are just Untermenschen, animals, vermin, roaches, lice;
- minimization—we don't torture, we just use enhanced interrogation techniques;
- the lie "we are not evil," therefore those we abuse must be guilty—a view that has its own internal combustion, feeding fuel for further atrocities. The worse I treat you, the guiltier and more horrible a person you must be.

Tavris and Aronson write:

> Self-justification has costs and benefits. By itself, it's not necessarily a bad thing. It lets us sleep at night. Without it, we would prolong the awful pangs of embarrassment. We would torture ourselves with regret over the road not taken or over how badly

we navigated the road we did take. We would agonize in the aftermath of almost every decision: Did we do the right thing, marry the right person, buy the right house, choose the best car, enter the right career? Yet mindless self-justification, like quicksand, can draw us deeper into disaster. It blocks our ability to even see our errors, let alone correct them. It distorts reality, keeping us from getting all the information we need and hindering our ability to clearly evaluate issues. It prolongs and widens rifts between lovers, friends, and nations. It keeps us from letting go of unhealthy habits. It permits the guilty to avoid taking responsibility for their deeds. And it keeps many professionals from changing outdated attitudes and procedures that can be harmful to the public.[53]

Self-justification is like dark chocolate—an essential ingredient for many of us to help cope with life, along with providing some health benefits. But gobs of it will seriously affect our health. And we eat too much of self-justification. When small or large disruptions recall something that is incongruent with how we view ourselves, the dissonance is unsettling, and instead of accepting the painful reality of "I was wrong," we often excuse ourselves. Like a sci-fi movie, we try to create an alternative universe with the same people but reset the timeline, magically erase the past, and hope everyone forgets what we did in this universe.

The problem has existed for ages. In the tale of Adam and Eve, Adam wasted no time telling God that the entire problem developed because of "the woman whom you gave to be with me" (Gen 3:12). After eating the forbidden fruit, Adam and Eve hide, blame, complain, accuse, defend, deceive, attack, and offer halfhearted admissions of wrongdoing.

Every day we hear these evasive maneuvers. Here are some I have either heard or used myself:

- "I was only kidding." (Didn't you get the joke?)
- "I was just being honest." (Can't you handle the truth?)
- "I didn't mean to do it." (I didn't think I'd get caught.)
- "It made me so angry." (Something else caused this blowup.)
- "I misunderstood you." (You're not as crazy as I thought.)
- "I'm just saying what I feel." (There is nothing wrong with my feelings.)
- "My family was like that." (If you think I'm bad, you should meet my . . .)

- "I'm having a dreadful day." (I deserve a break.)
- "I'm sorry, but you . . ." (It's really your fault.)
- "So? I made a mistake." (Don't we all, especially you?)
- "You misunderstood me." (I'm not as bad as that.)
- "Nobody's perfect." (Including you.)
- "That's just who I am." (Deal with it.)
- "I'm just upset." (The problem is that you don't care about me.)
- "We have a communication problem." (You're at least half the problem.)
- "You're just too sensitive." (It's not my fault you're prickly.)
- "I'm sorry I offended you, please forgive me." (You get easily offended.)
- "I'm not yelling!" (That's just how I talk.)

Houdini would be impressed. With the hidden key of self-justification we can unlock the straight jacket, chains, and locks, all while submerged upside down in a water tank, leaving our stunned audience trying to figure out what just happened. It's a brilliant con.

For example, by saying "I'm sorry I offended you, please forgive me," the word "sorry" is unassociated with anything I have done or said. "Sorry" is joined to a potential reaction on your part—you taking offense—a reaction that is beside the point. Or even better, "I'm sorry *if* I offended you." Now I leave you trying to decide whether you were offended, and, if so, what's the relevance. Then, with a sense of entitlement, I quickly move to begging for your forgiveness, once again putting the focus on you. In one blurt, I have ignored my faults, distracted you, pleaded for you to do something, and made it sound like I am terribly sorry. Q. E. D.

Too often, an apology is a tactic to admit the least as possible in order to get away with as much as possible. We have developed apologies into an art form. There are now "apology consultants" for criminal defendants charging up to $1000 an hour.[54] Of course, the word "sorry" can be genuine depending on the context; for instance, (1) Let me listen to your side. (2) You are right. (3) I was wrong. (4) I don't want to act like this. (5) I am sorry. (6) What can I do to fix this? Too often, however, we use the word with fancy footwork to get someone off our back or to recover a public image.

While gorging on self-justification, we end up feeling right about everything, which has further harmful consequences. When we are *right*:

- We struggle to listen. (Why listen when you already know the right answer?)
- We complain. (We know what is best and right.)
- We boast. (It feels great for others to see how right we are.)
- We defend ourselves. (People need regular reminders to show how right we are.)
- We are critical and harsh with others. (We are right about other people and their problems.)

No wonder change is hard and often requires a disruptive event to shake our certainties. Often there is a choice: insisting that we are right, or remaining in relationship. In such cases, we can either be right or be in relationship—but not at the same time.

The screen on our back door has a metal-sheet bottom. One night we had a violent storm with heavy winds. In the morning, I found our screen door smashed in, and was wondering what on earth had happened. Looking across to our neighbor's yard, I saw that a large tree close to our house had fallen. The tree was cut up and, in a few hours, carted off. The next day the stump was gone and covered over. But our door was smashed in, and I was convinced a large branch from the falling tree had bashed in our door.

We disliked this neighbor. The family had nicknamed her "Old Grumpy-Grouch." She was always doing sneaky things—like spraying weed-killer on our grass when it got too close to her fence, yelling at our kids to get off her lawn, puncturing balls, or taking and never returning toys that ended up in her yard—just the type of person who would conceal something like this. My wife Lori nonchalantly asked her, "Did your tree knock into our house?" The neighbor denied it. I thought Lori had gone soft on her. I was so convinced that I was itching to say something snarky to her like, "Did you happen to notice that your tree smashed up our door?" A couple of days later, I saw one of my sons crashing into the door with his bicycle—this had become his preferred and quick method of opening the door.

Relational failure

The Sith, in George Lucas' *Star Wars* universe, are quintessential examples of evil because they are out of relationship with everyone. Over the ages, there had been so much infighting between the Sith that by the end of the New Sith Wars, the Lord of the Sith, Darth Bane, instituted the "rule of two." Presumably to prevent the infighting, from now on there would be only *two* Sith—a master and an apprentice. But even this arrangement can't hold the forces of evil, and it doesn't take much for one to bump the other off.

Humanity also has its dark side. Trolls once only roamed the forests or basements of fiction, blundering brutes who could be quickly dispatched by Gandalf or three teen wizards. Now they are purveyors of toxicity on the internet, trashing, taunting, and taking delight in the suffering of others. And all for "laughs," whether it is trolling memorial sites for the dead or hacking websites to install epileptic patterns that generate seizures, and, of course, all combined with the requisite hatred toward women. Some have the "dark tetrad of personality"—narcissism, Machiavellianism, psychopathy, and sadism. And sadly, this is only one example of the darkness found in humankind.

Any discussion on the worthwhile life needs ways to speak about destructive ways of relating. In keeping with our aim of dialoguing with Christianity, we'll consider some ways Christianity has described this nasty side of human behavior—behavior that undermines the good and worthwhile life.

Christianity has traditionally spoken of "sin" to describe the dark side of humanity. But what is sin, and how do we know? Is "sin" even a helpful category to use today to describe harmful or evil human behavior? We have reason to be skeptical because the use of "sin" is often associated with silly people who rant about "sin" and how rotten everyone is, and who use their view of sin to exclude the "sinner," the outsider, and the rule-breaker who has violated the laws of their community. In this sense, talk of "sin" is simply a means to control the group and exclude dissenters.

In addition, to further control people, "sins" are often invented and multiplied to increase shame and guilt—whether it be no meat on Friday, no dancing on Saturday, or no TV on Sunday—while offering promises of absolution provided you stay in the group. Laws against these "sins" define the identity of the group and regulate behavior, and keep people enslaved to guilt (where they break the laws) and self-righteousness (where they keep them). Just think about how many churches attach "sins" to areas surrounding sex and gender, including homosexuality, masturbation, and especially with controlling women—their makeup, jewelry, clothes, perfume, relationships—and thus all the interminable rules for women: rules for submission; rules for speaking; rules for what level of intimacy before marriage (rules for hand holding, kissing, being alone in the same room, heavy petting, sex); rules that maintain a purity culture and idolize virginity; rules for whom they can marry; rules for not marrying a divorced person; rules for what birth control they can or cannot use; rules for jewelry (perhaps only in the ear and nowhere else); rules for clothes (height of skirts, only cotton underwear);

rules for the number of children they should have (usually a lot); rules that create the impression that sex is dirty or sinful.

Even if the word "sin" is going to be used today, how is it to be defined? Some look to tradition to describe sin. This may help, but often we find behavior that was once acceptable in the past is now abhorrent to us. Some look to the Bible. Again, we may find help, but among the good, we also find patriarchy, slavery, genocide, capturing and raping women in war, torture, forced marriages, polygamy, and death penalties for trivial offenses. There are plenty of behavior and commands in the Bible that we now consider immoral.

In addition, we find that even in the Bible, the way people understood "sin" underwent a transformation. Sin has a varied history. Views on sin have morphed according to the culture and what made sense at that time. Notre Dame Professor of Hebrew Bible Gary Anderson, in his book *Sin: A History*, shows this progression in the Bible. In the Hebrew Bible, a common metaphor for sin was of a weight or burden.[55] Sin was a burden to be carried, and therefore, on the Day of Atonement, sin could be carried by a scapegoat into the desert. By New Testament times, however, under Hellenistic economic influences, sin became understood as a debt. With this metaphor of debt came a different solution—removing the debt by some sort of payment. And the converse—if sin is a debt, then a virtuous act is a credit.

Views of sin continued to morph. By the time of the Reformation, following John Calvin (who was trained as a lawyer), the Reformed theological tradition placed a substantial emphasis on sin as a breaking of law. In contrast to Martin Luther, Calvin stressed the so-called third use of the law—that law was also direction for living the Christian life. Here, sin is conceived of as breaking the precepts and directions of the law. The stress on law is understandable given that the world was emerging from a context where the feudal lord or king could do whatever he wanted. The Reformation was followed by the legal codification of theology in the Westminster Confession of Faith (1646) and its catechisms that were long expositions of the Ten Commandments, and the appearances of books like the Puritan Samuel Rutherford's *Lex, Rex* (The law is king) (1644). By 1689, William and Mary became king and queen of England only after signing the Bill of Rights that placed the monarch under the rule of law. In many churches, the theme of law became all-embracing, oozing into every crevice. We still find this legal framework today in denominations and seminaries that are descendants of Calvin. These groups solve problems by "charges" (indictments) and church courts, and structure their theology in overarching legal frameworks; for example, sin and atonement are formulated in terms of law.

The way sin is conceived correlates with the solutions offered. If sin is a burden, then it can be carried away into the wilderness. If it is a debt, then it can be repaid or someone else can pay it. If sin is a breaking of law, the solution will be couched in a legal framework. Each view has its own peculiarities. For example, under a strict legal framework, God can't just forgive sins because the law requires obedience and punishment for disobedience.

In Christianity, sin has a history. Sin's meaning has changed. Sin has been variously described, among other things, as a burden, a debt, a breaking of law, as idolatry (that what we love is out of order), a corrupting substance within us, a missing of the mark, an evil power or demonic force over humanity, an absence of good, a stain or blemish, a deed against God, a breaking of *shalom*, or an act against nature, good order, or reason. In addition, through the history of Christianity, exactly what constitutes a sin has morphed. Is slavery a sin? Polygamy? What about women in church leadership? What about homosexuality?

If Christians are still going to use the word "sin" today, we need explanations of sin that make sense in the twenty-first century. Now, a redefinition shouldn't be a problem for Christians because Christianity has continually revised its understanding of sin. What metaphors make sense today? We have already talked about relational failure, and I will argue that placing sin under the rubric of *relational failure*[56] encompasses, expands, corrects, and surpasses prior notions of sin.

Connecting the Christian concept of "sin" to relational failure brings us to the twenty-first century, where the category of relationships has found remarkable traction and success. An emphasis on relational thinking has transformed diverse fields and disciplines, from the natural sciences to the social sciences to the humanities.

Relationships as reality

A remarkable change in the way people understand the world is how we now view relationships as the key to understanding reality. In contrast to the past, relationships are now central and primary. Across a large swath of disciplines—from linguistics, philosophy, theology, economics, psychology, mathematics, evolutionary biology, and other physical and social sciences, theories of relationships have redefined disciplines. Networks of relationships are now the novel way of conceptualizing reality—where relationships are not only real but are the underlying or greater reality.

We now hear of "neural networks," "computer networks," "gene networks," and societies defined as "networks of relationships." And the way these networks are structured gives rise to emergent properties—characteristics that differ from the individual parts. The realization that relationships are central and have emergent properties is a remarkable change in our understanding and perception of the world.

Philosophy has transformed from the ancient Greek stress on substance to the primacy of relationships. Both Plato and Aristotle privileged "substance" over "relationships." Relationships were secondary and didn't define an object or a person. Modern philosophy since Hegel and Kant has moved away from the primacy of substances and now stresses and privileges relationships.

Psychology and other social sciences now view people not as individual persons, but as beings-in-relationships. We now read books like Daniel Goleman's *Social Intelligence: The New Science of Human Relationships*,[57] and Matthew Lieberman's *Social: Why Our Brains Are Wired to Connect*,[58] which have helped popularize this new understanding. We now hear words such as *Ubuntu*, a favorite African word that is given the meaning: "I am only human in relation to you." There is increasing recognition that our beliefs are relationally determined. If you grew up with Hindu parents, it is more than coincidence that you became Hindu. What we determine to be real and true is decided by relationships. Our personalities are formed and defined by our relationships to others. This has important ramifications for change and growth. Want more self-control? Socialize with people with high self-discipline. A three-step plan to losing weight? Reduce calorie intake, cut out sugar and refined carbs, and hang out with some like-minded friends. Even better, tell your friends that you are committed to losing weight, which adds a motivating social contract.

In the biological sciences, there is the understanding that humankind is integrally connected to other species, not only in shared ecosystems but also through evolutionary development. Evolutionary theory, which includes diverse fields from paleontology to genetics, has connected all species relationally into a web of countless relationships and inter-connections.

This change to a relational understanding of our world is increasingly mirrored in theology. Like ancient philosophy, theology once also stressed substance over relations, as seen in the early church with a concern to emphasize that Jesus is one "substance" with the Father. Just as they privileged "substance," they also privileged "sameness" and these categories structured their theological formulations.[59] So in formulating the Nicene Creed, they debated whether Jesus was the "same substance" (*homoousios*) or a "similar substance" (*homoiousios*) with the Father. As you can see from the Greek transliteration, the difference was only one Greek letter: "i" (iota). In this case, it really mattered one iota. But such concerns sound strange to our ears. What makes more sense for Christians today, for example, is the revival of Trinitarian theology in the twentieth century—that God is relational and ultimate reality is about relationships.

In the physical sciences, John Dewey expressed this development by noting that modern science is not about objects but about relationships. Since Einstein, matter and energy are not viewed as separate things, but exist in relationship and can change from one into the other. Similarly, space and time exist in relationship. Einstein famously said that there is no ticking clock in the universe. Space and time are not absolute nor are they "things." What we think of as solid is mostly empty space, and the particles aren't solid ball-like objects. Particles are now probability waves—behaving like a wave and a particle—and matter results from these "particles" interacting with the Higgs field. In other words, matter forms through relationships. And in the quantum world, we find the remarkable and bizarre relationship of quantum entanglement—what Einstein dismissively called "spooky action at a distance"—where if you change something with a particle over here, its entangled particle, even if it is a billion miles away over there, immediately registers that change.

Even in fields that are not immediately obvious, the "turn to relationality"[60] is apparent. In linguistics, since Ferdinand de Saussure, we find a focus on the relationship between words rather than the words themselves; that we find meaning not in individual words but in the relationship of words—in sentences and paragraphs. Thus, language is a network of relationships. Even in mathematics, we can find examples. The most prolific mathematician of the twentieth century, Paul Erdös, the subject of the delightful book *The Man Who Loved Only Numbers*,[61] developed graph theory, which is now known as network theory. Suffice to say, we now know that everything in our universe is integrally connected, although we still struggle to explain these connections. In fact, an entire field of network science has arisen that studies the properties of physical, computer, biological, semantic, and social networks.

From these networks and relationships arise emergent properties. The structures of networks have characteristics independent of the individual parts. What materializes is difficult to guess from the constituent parts. For instance, sodium and chlorine are hazards by themselves. Some of us can recall pyrotechnic chemistry experiments where we fooled around with sodium—a metal that behaves itself when stored in oil but explodes when dropped in water. Likewise, chlorine is a noxious gas used as a poison in World War I. But put them together and we have table salt, an essential compound for our lives. The two constituent parts are lethal, but united they form a life-sustaining compound. A new reality emerges from the parts and the new relationship determines the properties.

Similarly, the arrangement of carbon atoms determines whether we have diamond, graphite, carbon nanotubes, or graphene—the strongest known material. Different arrangements of identical atoms have vastly different properties—either some of the hardest, softest, or strongest materials known. We find the property of emergence across fields, where the network has different properties from the constituent parts. Software as it crosses a hundred thousand lines of code can have emergent behavior. The cliché "computers only do what you tell them" doesn't consider behavior that can produce unintended results. Thus, with complex computer programs, there is the never-ending quest to find and squash bugs. The Internet, tax codes, and legal systems have emergent and unexpected properties that people can exploit. The economy and weather are all emergent systems that defy complete analysis. Our minds are an emergent property from a network of relationships—of some 86 billion neurons and 100 trillion connections—although no single neuron has any clue what is going on.

In addition, research is increasingly interdisciplinary and collaborative. More scholars are connecting across disciplines, avoiding insular thinking, where the temptation is to ignore other disciplines. We are now encouraged to understand how everything relates together. What is well known in one area is often unknown in another. Therefore, by forging new relationships, interdisciplinary work and conversation has incredible potential for creating something new and furthering understanding. By intentionally making connections and bringing one area of expertise and applying it to another, we create catalysts for innovative ideas.

Relationships now define what is real. Thus, in this present environment, understanding the dark side of humanity as "relational failure" makes sense and has many advantages.

One benefit of viewing sin as "relational failure" is that a relational understanding of sin encapsulates areas that Christians often separate; for instance, (1) a nasty comment, (2) the marginalization of women, and (3) the destruction of the environment. Christians usually view the first as sin, the second and third, not so much. All three, however, are relational failures and therefore sin. In this view, there is no gulf between individual, group, or environmental transformation. Sadly, in the church's list of the seven deadly sins (gluttony, sloth, envy, pride, anger, greed, and lust), we are missing the seven relational sins of bigotry, racism, misogyny, classism, xenophobia, homophobia, and environmental abuse. At the forefront today are two significant sins: the marginalization and abuse of women, and environmental despoliation—including toxic pollution, extinction of species, deforestation, global warming, and loss of biodiversity. A flourishing life is one that enables other species to flourish as well, including the female half of the human species.[62]

Another benefit is that sin as relational failure keeps us from the quick and easy attribution of the other person as the "sinner." Other conceptions of sin, such as sin as a breaking of the law, easily lend themselves to attributing someone else as a lawbreaker. In a relational view, we are involved with the "other," and may well be a significant contributor to relational failure with those outside our community. With any relationship, it is more likely "we have sinned." Problems between two people or between two nations are rarely the fault of just one.

Legal systems

Cults, religions, and political systems are often mired in legal systems, where rules and regulations are front and center. These legal systems often hinder the good life. Legal views of "sin" and laws regulating behavior can only take us so far and sometimes encourage the dark side of humanity. Sometimes, the law is like a big fishing net that easily catches a benign dolphin but has difficulty ensnaring piranhas that can shred a person to the bone in minutes.

Although "the rule of law" is an excellent progression in the growth and stability of human societies, laws cannot solve all our problems and are sometimes counterproductive or harmful. In the sixth century BCE, the philosopher Anacharsis remarked that laws are like spider webs that catch the weak and poor but are easily broken by the mighty and rich. Aristotle, who valued the rule of law, also emphasized that one needs practical wisdom and good character to interpret these laws fairly. Ernst Fraenkel reflects these ideas in his theory of the dual state—where one side of the state enforces the laws, while the other side is free from the law. In a dual state, the laws are for the little people, the minorities, the poor and disadvantaged, and not for Wall Street, government officials, CEOs, the CIA, architects of war and torture, or the rich who can afford high-price defense attorneys. In such a state, "justice" is increasingly only available to those who can afford it or those who know the "right" people.

We only have to picture a sign saying "Whites Only" to know that laws can often promote and enforce evil. Apartheid and slavery were once both "legal." Feminists, blacks, and gays have long noted how legal systems favor men, whites, and heterosexuals. These systems often fail women, especially in stalking, harassment, abuse, and rape cases. Even when women go to *law enforcement*, they often suffer more abuse, victim blaming, or stonewalling.

Returning to Hugo's *Les Misérables*: The police inspector Javert has relentlessly pursued Jean Valjean, whose original crime was only stealing some food to feed his family. Many years later, after Valjean has rebuilt his life, he is discovered and recaptured by Javert. Hugo describes the scene:

> Javert was in seventh heaven at that moment. Without being distinctly aware of it, yet with a vague intuition of his indispensability and his success, he, Javert, personified justice, light, and truth in their heavenly capacity for crushing evil. Behind and around him, reaching to infinite depths, he had authority, reason, a definitive verdict, legal integrity, the vindication of public morality, every star in his favor. He was protecting order, delivering the law's thunderbolt, avenging society; he was the enforcer of the absolute. He rode on a cloud of glory . . . Rejoicing and indignant, under his heel he crushed crime, vice, rebellion, damnation, hell.[63]

Had Javert ever felt more alive and important? Javert's sentiment is captured in the musical version of *Les Misérables* where he sings with gusto about the law-abiding and unchanging stars in the sky, that those who fall will pay the price. Javert is the consummate moralist whose words capture a "theology of exclusion"—only the law-abiding will enter heaven, all the rest will pay dearly (and I will feel great). You die and I live. Javert is a legalist—one who uses and abuses a legal system to cover his depravity and to achieve personal power and glory. He is a moralist who leaves a trail of death and destruction, a crazed pit bull who never lets go until there is a bloody mess on the floor.

Our ethical sensibilities are now more cautious of legal systems as an overarching solution for human flourishing. They are no longer a panacea, the way to solve all problems, and sometimes cause further evil. We can't regulate many things, including mercy and common sense. But we continue to throw laws at problems. For example, the draconian three-strike law in California ensnared the thirty-three-year-old black man, Curtis Wilkerson. Wilkerson was caught stealing socks worth $2.50 from a mall store—the offense was so small that the store security officials debated whether to call the police. But police were called, and because Wilkerson had two prior convictions, for this third offense, he subsequently received twenty-five years to life.[64] For stealing a pair of white socks, Wilkerson wouldn't be eligible for parole for twenty-five years. Javert would be impressed. Prohibition is another example. The Eighteenth Amendment to the US Constitution to prohibit alcohol (the only amendment to be repealed) is now considered a catastrophic failure, and the results were overwhelmingly negative—failing to cure the problem, draining government resources, snowballing corruption, increasing violence, and creating vicious national crime syndicates. These results lead many to make the comparison between Prohibition and the current misguided war on drugs.

A relational approach supports the use and the value of laws for successful communities, but questions religious groups that define "sin" as a breaking of law, or communities with unjust legal systems, or nations that view "laws" as the answer to every problem.

For instance, one "sin" in many religious communities is stipulated by the rule "do not gossip." With a little thought, however, we can find value in gossip. Gossip can be nasty, but gossip is often beneficial social glue, and the grapevine can protect a community from cheats, crazies, frauds, and predators. Much gossip is neutral or positive. Gossip can clarify and solidify moral behavior and promote cooperation among those oppressed. It can help form bonds and spread useful information. In addition, churches and seminaries are no strangers to abusive leaders who use rules against gossip to cover their tracks and stifle dissent. A relational approach still upholds the "spirit of the law" and discourages malicious gossip, but allows for many circumstances when gossiping is fine, even the right thing to do. Often the clearness and definiteness of a legal approach is a mirage, where once you arrive you discover you haven't reached the oasis of relational harmony.

Or, as another example, some moral philosophers debate whether the stipulation "do not lie" is the right thing to do in every circumstance. The famous example is where the Gestapo arrive at the front door of your house. You are hiding Jews in the attic. What should you say? Should you lie or tell the truth? The chances that we would be in such a moral quandary are remote. But for what it is worth, legal approaches would usually say, "Never lie under any circumstance." Some, however, may allow for a more ingenious approach, where you still tell the "truth," but your statement is intended to distract and mislead, "I saw some Jews in town yesterday, but I haven't seen them today." Are we doomed to promote wrongdoing—either by lying or by telling the truth and thus exposing those under our care? Truthfulness in relationships is vital, but a legal approach usually entertains no exceptions, nuance, flexibility, or the possibility that following the "law" is committing an atrocity. With a relational approach, of course you lie to protect the innocent from genocidal psychopaths. The lie allows you to stay in faithful relationship with those you are hiding, robs the Gestapo of committing further evil, and allows you to live with yourself. Of course, even in the Bible, there are examples of justified lying, such as the midwives lying to Pharaoh (Exod 1:18–21) and Rahab lying about Joshua's spies (Josh 2:4–6; Jas 2:25).

The rule "do not lie" is usually the right thing to do, and directives such as these have traction, not because of the supremacy of law, but because truth-telling is essential to the foundation of relationships—trust. And sometimes the most successful lies are telling the "precise truth" that excludes other realities. A relational approach takes us much further in the quest for the good life, whereas legal approaches cannot capture many deceptions and exceptions.

Understanding the dark side of human behavior as relational failure exposes legal approaches as inadequate. It is quite easy to follow a set of rules and be a horrible person. Laws can provide cover and justification for the most horrific acts. Countless people have been morally certain about their views of slaves, women, witches, infidels, heretics, homosexuals, honor killings of daughters, and wife beatings. Moral certainty and legal solutions are overrated.

> Never let your sense of morals get in the way of doing what is right.
>
> —Isaac Asimov[65]

Emergent properties of relational failure

When studying relationships, we discover emergent properties. Speaking of "relational failure," we can also talk about the emergent properties of evil. A case in point: the ongoing discussion on Hitler's National Socialism. How could this happen in Germany—the land of Bach, Beethoven, Brahms, Schiller, and Goethe—the country with the highest literacy rate in the world and at the forefront of scientific research? Historians agree "no Hitler, no Holocaust," but Hitler managed to whip massive crowds into an extraordinary madness and delusion, and he had a knack for finding and exploiting weaknesses and the basest characteristics in others.

Can relational failure have emergent properties quite different and unpredictable from the constituent parts? In a relational view, some great evils are an emergent complexity—where the arrogance, greed, hatred, and lust of a collective group amalgamates and morphs into a deeper perversity, producing evils such as genocide, ethnic cleansing, sex trafficking, environmental destruction, or institutionalized pedophilia. Relational failure may have emergent properties that we cannot predict from the individual parts. The discrete parts—the social and political upheaval in Germany, the economic catastrophe because of war reparations, the humiliation after Versailles, the centuries of antisemitism, Hitler's cronies—Goebbels, Himmler, Bormann, Goering, Heydrich, and even Hitler himself (including his supposedly one testicle, abusive father, stinging rejection by the Vienna Academy of Fine Arts, or chronic drug use)—doesn't explain or account for the whole emergent phenomenon that was Nazi Germany and the Holocaust. It is unexplainable from the parts precisely because emergent evil is unpredictable from the constituent parts. Just as we cannot guess table salt from sodium and chlorine, so there is no satisfying answer to be found from examining the individual pieces of Nazi Germany.

Hitler is a necessary but insufficient cause for the evil and madness of Nazi Germany. Primo Levi recounts an incident after his arrival at Auschwitz in his classic *If This Is a Man*.[66] In attempting to quench his thirst, Levi breaks off an icicle hanging from a window. A patrolling guard, however, sees him and snatches the ice away. Levi asks "Why?" The guard's response is "Here there is no why," a statement that seems to cover all the discrete parts of Nazi Germany. But looking at the whole emergent phenomena, we can say this is reason enough—humanity can and has committed these horrendous atrocities. And to say there is no explanation is to hide from our relational humanity with all its flaws.

The Parable of the Prodigal Son

Returning to our dialog with Christianity, viewing sin as "relational failure" can aid those within Christianity who in the twenty-first century want to promote the good life. Like other views of sin—burden, debt, legal—a relational understanding finds resonance within the New Testament. For readers who may wonder whether the idea of "sin" as relational failure has any basis in the Bible, consider one famous example that illustrates a relational view of sin.

The Parable of The Prodigal Son is the most famous parable, one of the greatest short stories, and a good example because many believe that this story captures the heart of Christianity. The parable follows the ever popular "rebellion—ruin—redemption" narrative arc. The Prodigal runs away from home, abandons his father and older brother, and squanders his inheritance. Of the two sons in the parable, the Prodigal's sins are obvious. He cares only for himself; he takes the money and runs. He rejects his significant relationships. Only after becoming destitute does the Prodigal return home to the open arms of his waiting father.

But what about the other son—the elder son who stays at home and apparently does nothing wrong? When the prodigal son returns home, everyone celebrates except the elder son. When the prodigal arrives home, the elder son is working in the field, doing his duty. He never deserted his loved ones nor wasted his father's money. But once he hears his brother has returned, and that there is a grand soiree, he is fuming and refuses to join in.

Philip Yancey tells the story of a pastor, Fred Craddock, who gave a sermon on this parable, but made a few changes to the story along the way. After the Prodigal came home, what did the father do? He slipped the ring on the elder son, and he killed the fattened calf in honor of his elder son—for all his years of arduous work and faithfulness. And a woman at the back of the church yelled out, "That's the way it *should* have been written!"[67]

Is the elder son just as lost as the younger Prodigal? The answer depends on how we view sin. If we consider sin as simply a breaking of the rules, then the elder son appears obedient. The sinner is the Prodigal who broke the law. But the elder son kept the rules and did what he was told.

With a relational view of sin, however, there is a problem with the elder son. He is estranged from his father and brother. We see the relational disconnect in his anger, condemnation, isolation, and manner of speaking. He tells his father, "All these years I have been *slaving* for you." His work is slavery and doesn't come from a relationally connected and free life. And when he refers to his brother, he doesn't say "my brother," but says to his father, "this son of yours."

The elder son is angry, refuses to join the party, and points the finger of disgust and condemnation. New Testament scholars have long observed that the story makes sense when viewed in its context in Luke's Gospel. Why did Jesus tell this story of the Prodigal Son? If we back up a bit to the beginning of the chapter, we read that tax collectors and sinners were coming to hear Jesus speak. The riffraff was gathering around Jesus, wanting to listen to him. But others—the religious leaders—were grumbling and muttering to themselves about how this fellow Jesus welcomes sinners and eats with them. In response, Jesus tells three parables—all about something being lost. The first parable is about a lost sheep. The second is about a lost coin. And here in the third story we have two lost sons. Here in the third parable, the elder son is lost, even though he still physically lives at home. The implication is that the elder son represents the religious leaders who are grumbling about these sinners with whom Jesus enjoys partying.

There are two lost sons and two different manifestations of sin. The one relational failure is technicolored and obvious. The other is allusive, hard to see, and deceptive because it sometimes looks good on the outside. Sin is far more encompassing than "law-breaking," reaching below the external appearance and reaching out to our relationships. With Jesus' portrayal of the elder son comes a sharp critique of the religious leaders—against their judgmental postures, their lack of self-awareness, and their deep relational failures.

* * *

The way Christianity conceives of sin has far-reaching consequences. If sin is a substance—something we are made of—how is it possible to change? By what alchemy can we transform the lead of substantive sin into gold? In addition, thinking of sin as a substance is often linked to the related category of "sameness." If sin is a substance, and substances tend not to change, then there is little hope of change, supporting the excuse, "That's just the way I am, so deal with it." We are now doomed to a Sisyphean task, where any progress is thwarted by our substantive sin that always drags us down to the bottom to start all over again.

These difficulties evaporate with relational understandings of sin. Relational change is possible and can happen swiftly. Central themes of relational transformation such as forgiveness or repentance are powerful because they transform relationships; that is, they deal with relational failure—with sin.

The central figure of Christianity, Jesus himself, redefines sin by socializing with "sinners." By enjoying the company of sinners, Jesus exposes the "righteous" view on sin. The experts in the law quickly defined Jesus as a "sinner," as one who was not kosher regarding the law. The irony is palpable—the experts of the *law* label Jesus the *sinner*. According to the Gospel of Mark, the religious leaders are apoplectic because Jesus heals on the Sabbath (Mark 3), and they immediately leave and plot to kill him. The "righteous" go forth to commit, according to their own law, the most terrible of crimes, which again shows the weakness of legal systems. But here is the catch: as with many who commit evil, they feel justified and righteous. After all, they were experts in their own law. They would have read about Phinehas who was *commended* by God for his zeal (Num 25:11) after Phinehas had killed a fraternizing Israelite and a Midianite woman. They would have read about the man stoned to death for picking up sticks on the Sabbath (Num 15:32–36) and God's instruction to put to death anyone who worked on the Sabbath (Exod 31:12–17). Who is this Jesus anyway? Our text nowhere tells us that an unknown carpenter, who skirts around the law, is in fact the Messiah.

Thus, there are views of sin that encourage relational harm rather than identify it. In this sense, some religious people have sinful views of sin—who through their theology and laws promote an "us-versus-them" dynamic that undermines the good life and categorizes people in order to judge and dismiss them.

Repentance, forgiveness, and the life worth living

Repentance

The word "repentance" (like "sin") has a bad name, often for good reasons. Sometimes the word conjures up images of a grimacing preacher with "repent" spewing from his lips, or a person yelling on the street and holding a sign saying "repent," or the outward reformation of a person after being punished or threatened with damnation, or a person sitting in a confessional divulging her secrets, or a Christian explaining what a miserable sinner he is.

Religious groups are known to use "repentance" to control and exploit their members. In *Going Clear: Scientology, Hollywood, and the Prison of Belief*, Lawrence Wright describes Scientologists exploiting taped confessions of its members, even to the extent of leaders reviewing tapes and laughing about them.[68] In some Christian groups, "repentance" is an identity marker of the group. Morose introspection and confession are group currency, elevating those who exhibit the best "repentance" to paragons of humility and insightfulness. To keep the system churning over, the group must find more and more sins to feed the confessional grinder. Repentance is now a duty, an art, and a means to signal group solidarity.

In addition, all too often, repentance is misapplied and used as a weapon against victims. Now the victim needs to repent. "Your husband abused you . . . Well, what were you doing?" "You were raped . . . Well, we heard rumors you were drinking and wearing suggestive clothing. You need to change."

Despite the abuse, however, we can argue that the word "repentance" is still useful when redefined relationally. Even if we decide to use another word, I will argue that the idea behind "repentance" is essential for transforming relationships and the good life.

The Bible even emphasizes this connection between repentance and the life worth living. In the biblical stories, those that live a repentant life are those who are transforming and pursuing the good life. A major theme running through the Hebrew Bible and New Testament connects repentance and the good life. Some examples:

It is the humble that God saves and sustains (2 Sam 22:28; Ps 147:6). God gives grace to the humble (Prov 3:34; Jas 4:6; 1 Pet 5:5–6). The one who repents finds mercy (Prov 28:13). The prophets Jeremiah and Ezekiel connect repentance with life and restoration (Jer 15:19; Ezek 18:32). For Isaiah, God dwells with and revives the humble (Isa 57:15). The promise at the end of Isaiah is that "he will come to Zion as Redeemer, to those in Jacob who turn from transgression" (Isa 59:20). And in the New Testament Gospels, a call to repentance accompanies the announcement of the coming kingdom. People are urged to produce fruit worthy of repentance (Matt 3:8) and do deeds that are consistent with repentance (Acts 26:20). We read that whoever humbles themselves is the greatest in the kingdom (Matt 18:4). At the start of the New Testament church, Peter connects repentance with the gift of the Holy Spirit (Acts 2:38), and at Solomon's porch Peter calls all people to repent, so their sins may be wiped out and refreshing times may come (Acts 3:19–20). Paul speaks of repentance as leading to salvation (2 Cor 7:10) and in 2 Timothy 2:25 we see repentance connected with a knowledge of the truth. And for a last example, in 1 John 1:9, we read, "If we confess our sins, he who is faithful and just will forgive us our sins and cleanse us from all unrighteousness."

In the biblical stories, there is a direct connection between repentance and an ethical life. Repentance brings life, mercy, knowledge of the truth, virtuous deeds, cleansing, grace, forgiveness, restoration, and the presence of God.

Some in the church's history have drawn attention to repentance. In 1517, Martin Luther started the Reformation by nailing his ninety-five theses on the door of his church in Wittenberg. The first thesis stated, "When our Lord and Master, Jesus Christ, said 'repent,' he meant that the entire life of believers should be one of repentance." Dietrich Bonhoeffer's famous phrase "cheap grace" in his *The Cost of Discipleship* was applied to those who downplayed repentance.[69] Rowan Williams, former archbishop of Canterbury, suggested adding a fifth mark of the church to the four in the Creed—a church that is one, holy, catholic, apostolic, and *repentant*.[70]

But like disruption, the emphasis on repentance catalyzing the good life is a neglected theme in Christian practice and theory. In practice, churches have often failed to lead as a community that is quick to shun self-justification and model repentance. The world knows the church more for calling others to repent, rather than being an example to follow. In theory, when Christians discuss how relational transformation occurs, there is often an emphasis on the various "means of grace" or "spiritual disciplines" or admonitions to "follow the law," which may include Bible reading, prayer, fasting, church attendance, taking the Lord's Supper, or obeying various rules and regulations—all to the neglect of repentance. It is a curious fact that many writings on the Christian life fail to stress repentance. In fact, the stories about Jesus have him rebuking people for reading the Scriptures yet missing out on him (John 5:39), empty and repetitious prayer (Matt 6:7), fasting to put on a show (Matt 6:16–18), and tithing while neglecting justice (Luke 11:42). Obviously, something else is needed. The biblical stories are clear—repentance is the means of grace, the catalyst for change. Repentance brings transformation and offers hope for everyone.

In the Harry Potter series, the question is asked whether the antagonist Voldemort can ever change. Voldemort, in a quest to conquer death, has managed (through murdering others) to rip his soul into seven pieces—and hidden each part of his soul in a secret item called a Horcrux.

At the beginning of the seventh book, *The Deathly Hallows*, Harry, Hermione, and Ron have a discussion about Voldemort. Ron wonders whether Voldemort could ever put his soul back together. Hermione replies that it would be possible, but excruciatingly painful. But by what process? The only way for Voldemort to put himself back together would be through remorse and really to feel what he had done.[71]

At the end of that book and of the entire series, in the last battle between Harry and Voldemort in the Great Hall, before Voldemort is killed by his own rebounding curse, Harry urges him to have remorse, offering one last chance to change. The narrator notes that of all the things that Harry had said to Voldemort, nothing shocked Voldemort as much as Harry's call for some remorse.[72]

The Harry Potter series offers the possibility for the arch villain, even after all he has done, to change and show some remorse—to feel even a little of the horror he inflicted. As we know, Voldemort didn't repent. For him, showing remorse would be a sign of weakness and impotence—a sign of defeat and undoing.

This illustrates one of the many challenges facing a discussion on repentance. People often view repentance as a sign of weakness and failure. In reality, our destructive behavior shows weakness and failure. A genuine apology is the opposite. It is a sign of strength of character and humility—an overcoming of the tremendous forces of our protective, blame-shifting, and self-justifying ways. Laozi in the Daodejing summarizes:

> Those who know others are knowledgeable;
> Those who know themselves are enlightened.
> Those who conquer others have power;
> Those who conquer themselves are strong.[73]

Being vulnerable and owning up is a strength and source of creative growth. Bridled and limited regret is a good thing. It shows that we are learning from our past mistakes and failures and are eager to be different. But we have few examples to follow. How many politicians show remorse? What corporate cultures encourage owning up to mistakes? Who among the religious elite are known for saying "we were wrong"? A church leader once told me that in the eight years of working at a church he had never heard the pastor once say he was sorry about anything. Our culture encourages us to dismiss regret, defend ourselves, find someone else to blame, move on, and hope no one notices or remembers.

In addition, another challenge facing a discussion on repentance is that it is often difficult to distinguish between fake and genuine repentance. Deception is . . . well . . . deceptive. Like psychopaths who learn how to mimic empathy, repentance can be mimicked. Talk about repentance is not repentance. Repentance has little to do with regaling an audience, priest, or person unrelated to the event in question. In fact, Pinker notes that "when people with antisocial personality disorder were asked to compose and deliver a speech about their own faults, which for ordinary people is a nerve-racking ordeal accompanied by embarrassment, shame, and guilt, their nervous systems were unresponsive."[74] Confessing our misdeeds to others while ignoring the person we harmed is not repentance, but a way to self-atone and self-inflate, and for some this public confession is apparently quite easy to do.

Like "sin," we can rescue the idea of repentance through a relational grid and it is too important a concept to let flounder. The following words illustrate and unpack what I mean by repentance:

Realize: Through disruption, we come to a new understanding and awareness of our surrounding reality. It shouldn't be so difficult! A genuine apology is simply recognizing and admitting what is true—what is true about ourselves. Once the cacophony of excuses dies down, we can listen to what our conscience or someone else is trying to tell us.

God laments in Jeremiah 8:6, "No one repents of wickedness, saying, 'What have I done!'" A new realization can lead to questioning: Is this who I want to be? They may be questions asked by an addict at rock-bottom: What is so desperate and tragic about my life that this addiction stirs "life" in me? What pain am I numbing? What about all the relationships I have harmed, the time I have wasted, my body I have damaged? How has it kept me from productive work and from improving this world? They may be questions asked by the narcissist at the end of his rope: How has this arrogance, insecurity, and selfishness turned me into a wraith or dementor, where I suck the life out of people instead of giving it? What can I possibly say to other people that is life-giving—that is not just mere words and lies? Or they may just be the simple questions: What can I change or do today that will help me on a worthwhile path? Am I spending my time on the right things?

Repentance includes self-realization, a coming to one's senses that dissolves excuses, exemplified in John Newton's "Amazing Grace": "Once I was blind, but now I see," in the Prodigal Son who eventually comes to his senses, or in King David who is cut to the heart after he realizes the evil he has committed.

Regret and Remorse: Regret has the idea that we are distressed about what happened. It also involves imagination—we feel regret when we imagine a different and better outcome. It is a good start, but often implies a sense of detachment. In addition, we need some remorse where we are personally sorry for having caused or contributed to the event. Remorse can then lead to ownership.

Responsibility: This was me. I'm going to do something about this. For example, in Luke 19:8, the tax collector Zacchaeus pledges to pay back fourfold everything that he has stolen. Responsibility is being accountable, having a sense of "I accept I did that. I dislike how I acted, and I want to be different." The world is still waiting, with little hope, for the Roman Catholic Church to repent over the child abuse scandal—in what is surely one of the greatest evils to tarnish Christianity. Where is the repentance to match the scope and horror of these crimes against humanity? Where is the outrage from the pews to force accountability? For decades, and perhaps centuries, abusive priests were shifted around, their crimes hidden, and given the opportunity for further abuse. And this wasn't the doing of a few rotten eggs. Thousands of priests have been implicated. Then there are the untold number of victims. We have heard plenty of excuses, but nothing like "We are slowly realizing the enormity of our crimes and we now want full accountability. We will invite an outside, independent investigation that will have access to all requested records and personnel. We will try to locate every victim and make reparations, even if it costs the wealth of the church. We are so horrified and ashamed that we will refrain from making moral judgements about others outside our community. And, we will long reflect on how our theological and organizational culture contributed to these evils and do whatever it takes to ensure it never happens again." Stating it like this shows the considerable cost involved in repentance, and the energy required to fight against what feels like dissolution. Great sins require great repentance.

Return: The word *return* captures the essence of repentance. In fact, one of the most frequently used words in the Hebrew Bible for repentance is *shuv*, a word for "turn." Repentance is not groveling in the dust in self-pity, nor is it mumbling "I'm sorry, but . . ." It is simply turning back, the concrete vulnerable movement toward the person or persons we have harmed.

With the idea of "turn," repentance can also have a more nuanced meaning—a turning away from supporting oppression and exploitation. Slaves, women, and LGBTQ persons have sometimes co-opted the views of their oppressors and supported slave-based, patriarchal, and homophobic cultures. For example, a woman who supports patriarchy could turn away, or repent, by renouncing this sexual oppression.

The Prodigal Son illustrates this turning. It is one thing for him to recognize his predicament and have remorse, but he also must leave the pigsty and return home to his family. Some have argued that the Parable of the Prodigal Son is not an illustration of repentance because it was only dire circumstances that led to his change. Well, exactly! Many of us usually only turn around when reality hits us over the head. Often, it is precisely when we are exposed that we wake up and come to our senses. Thus, the Prodigal is repentant, though imperfect. He turns around and goes back. King David is brought to repentance only when Nathan enters his palace and disrupts David with a parable that exposes his murder and adultery. It is only after being in captivity that Manasseh prays and humbles himself (2 Chr 33:11–13). Jonah repents after spending three days in a fish! The thief on the cross next to Jesus, amid his suffering, exhibits some repentance. Without some disruption, we usually continue on our merry way.

We find a historical example of the power of repentance in the life of the Puritan Samuel Sewall (1652–1730), a judge who presided over the Salem witch trials.[75] After the trials had come to an ignominious end and twenty people had been sent to their deaths, Sewall was cut to the heart and publicly repented for his role—the only judge to do so. His subsequent life showed a remarkable transformation with his concern for slaves, Native Americans, and women. After his public apology in 1697, Sewall turned his attention to the plight of slaves. In 1700 he wrote and published *The Selling of Joseph*,[76] the first abolitionist tract printed in America. Sewell went on to champion the rights of Native Americans and women during a time when most considered them savages or inferior. His essay "Talitha Cumi"[77] argued that both women's and men's bodies would be raised in the resurrection, contrary to the widespread belief that everyone would be raised male and that heaven would be male. It is remarkable to read an article written by a man in 1724 that begins with Galatians 3:28, "There is no longer male and female; for all of you are one in Christ Jesus," and ends by speaking of the rights of women. It is even more remarkable given Sewell's past.

Repentance is a reorientation of our lives, involving a return to the person we hurt, with a refreshing lack of excuses—a movement requiring great strength. The result is humility and a healing relationship. Humility is not something we can drum up or buy from the local café. It is simply a result of repentance and a realization that we don't deserve special treatment. Humility is the carbon dioxide of a repentant life, a byproduct. Try to attain it or claim it (breathe it in), it is toxic, leading to hypocrisy. After repentance, we find we have more inner strength and gain hope in our ability to improve our relationships. And to extend the analogy, just as carbon dioxide feeds the growth of trees and plants, so does this humility—a vital component for the good life—feed the good growth of society.

Forgiveness

Any relationship will face failures; thus, to continue to live in healthy relationships and to pursue the good life with others, we need at least two things—repentance (for our own relational failures) and forgiveness (for the relational failures of others). Repentance and forgiveness are the two neutralizers for the acid of sin. Repentance addresses our sins; forgiveness addresses the sins of others; and maintaining healthy relationships requires both.

We find an example of the power of forgiveness to encourage the good life in South Africa's Truth and Reconciliation Commission. Archbishop Desmond Tutu, the chairperson of that committee, in *No Future without Forgiveness*,[78] describes the work and goals of the committee. How was South Africa to deal with the brutal past of apartheid? What approach could help prevent South Africa from descending into a bloodbath of racial hatred? Was there a way forward that would encourage restorative justice rather than retributive justice?

Tutu explains how the country chose a "third way." One way would be to go the route of the Nuremberg trials, a legal approach, where perpetrators of crimes against humanity would be tried and sentenced. Another way would be to sweep everything under the carpet, start afresh, and ignore the huge piles of dirt under the rug that would cause people to trip.

A third option, which South Africa chose, was the way of accountability and forgiveness. The commission would give victims an opportunity to tell their stories and be eligible for reparations. Perpetrators would be given amnesty for politically motivated crimes, provided they fully disclosed their crimes. Those who didn't request or receive amnesty faced prosecution and imprisonment.[79] The commission gave opportunities for people to express remorse and to offer forgiveness. In addition, many crimes that would have remained unsolved were exposed and victims found out what really happened to their relatives. For example, in 1988, Khotso House, the headquarters for the South African Council of Churches in downtown Johannesburg, was destroyed by a massive bomb. The Minister of Law and Order, Adriaan Vlok, announced the ANC had planted the bomb. The police even arrested and detained without trial the person whom they said was responsible, the political activist Shirley Gunn. Later, when Vlok applied for amnesty, he admitted before the commission that he had (from instructions from the then-State President P. W. Botha) ordered the police to plant the explosives, and then apologized to Gunn for falsely accusing her.

The country's first democratically elected president, Nelson Mandela, also admirably modeled forgiveness. Mandela, who had ample reasons for bitterness and revenge, chose to forgive, exemplified by inviting his former prison guard to his inauguration and visiting the widow of the architect of apartheid, Betsy Verwoerd. Desmond Tutu has taken this message of forgiveness as a hopeful solution to Ireland, Israel, Rwanda, and elsewhere. Of course, the path of forgiveness is hard. The commission wasn't perfect. Not everyone expressed remorse or gave forgiveness, but many did. It was messy and risky, but that is the reality of relationships.

Tutu makes it explicit that his Christianity informed and directed his leadership of the commission. We see the centrality of forgiveness in Christianity in Jesus' words on the cross, "Father, forgive them; for they do not know what they are doing" (Luke 23:34) and in one of Jesus' more famous parables on the Unmerciful Servant (Matt 18:21–35). The occasion for that parable is Peter asking Jesus the question, "How many times must I forgive? As many as seven times?" Peter's question reflects the wariness we often have regarding forgiveness. How often should I forgive this person? What if she keeps on doing the same thing? Is there a limit to forgiveness? Part of the difficulty with forgiveness is that it feels like we will become a doormat upon which people will continue to wipe their feet. Is forgiveness a weakness that opens us for further abuse? In this parable, Jesus describes a man who owed ten thousand talents to a king.[80] The man is brought before the king, and because he cannot pay this enormous debt, the king orders that the servant and his family be sold into slavery. The servant begs for mercy, and the king has pity on him, forgiving the entire debt.

There are many descriptions and definitions of forgiveness, but in this parable, forgiveness is described in terms of bookkeeping. The king goes to check his account books. Does everything balance? No, but he wipes the books clean. He takes the loss upon himself, forgives everything, with no fine print.

Forgiveness seems difficult and unfair. How can we simply cancel abuse, betrayal, and other harms and hurts? The temptation is to make perpetrators pay—make them pay back *everything* they owe—then we will cancel the debt! Compounding the problem are situations where victims are revictimized by being urged to forgive, when all they feel is appropriate anger. Many church leaders have short-circuited the healing process by insisting that victims forgive and move on. In addition, the perpetrator may use a plea for forgiveness to make themselves feel better, while exhibiting self-justification and little remorse.

But as time goes on and after further reflection, the value of forgiveness, like a late spring after a bleak winter, can bring new hope and life. Eric Lomax in *The Railway Man: A POW's Searing Account of War, Brutality and Forgiveness* describes his dreadful treatment as a Japanese POW in World War II. The abuse he suffered is almost indescribable. On one occasion, Lomax received a beating that broke his teeth, broke both forearms, cracked several ribs, damaged his hip, and his back was so severely beaten that no white skin was left—all was blue and black.[81] On other occasions he was waterboarded. Lomax and other POWs were forced to stand at attention for twelve hours in the sun, with no water.[82] They were kept in cages in the yard, about five feet long, five feet tall, and two and a half feet wide, cells that became like ovens in the heat.

After the war and upon returning home, he heard that his mother had died three and a half years before, believing that her son was dead. Then there were the nightmares, difficulties adjusting, desires for vengeance against the Japanese, and a marriage that eventually collapsed. Revenge was on his mind for many years. Lomax remarried and eventually embarked on a quest to find out more about what happened in captivity and the identities of his captors. He came across an article on a person named Nagase Takashi who had now devoted his life to atone for Japanese treatment of POWs and was now working for reconciliation. Lomax recognized Nagase as one particularly nasty interrogator who summed up all the abuse Lomax had suffered. Remarkably, after some correspondence, it was clear that Nagase was a changed man, and they finally agreed to meet at Kanburi, where Lomax had been imprisoned, now some fifty years later. Lomax describes the meeting:

> He [Nagase] looked at me; he was trembling, in tears, saying over and over "I am very, very sorry . . ." I somehow took command, led him out of the terrible heat to a bench in the shade; I was comforting him, for he was really overcome. At that moment my capacity for reserve and self-control helped me to help him, murmuring reassurances as we sat down. It was as though I was protecting him from the force of the emotions shaking his frail-seeming body. I think I said something like "That's very kind of you to say so" to his repeated expressions of sorrow.

He said to me, "Fifty years is a long time, but for me it is a time of suffering. I never forgot you, I remember your face, especially your eyes." He looked deep into my eyes when he said this . . .[83]

Before Lomax returned to England, he gave Nagase a letter, which he describes:

I read my short letter out to him, stopping and checking that he understood each paragraph. I felt he deserved this careful formality. In the letter I said that the war had been over for almost fifty years; that I had suffered much; and that I knew that although he too had suffered throughout this time, he had been most courageous and brave in arguing against militarism and working for reconciliation. I told him that while I could not forget what happened in Kanburi in 1943, I assured him of my total forgiveness.[84]

Lomax and his wife—who had accompanied him on the trip—wondered for a moment whether they did the right thing. Yes. Lomax ends his book with the words he said to his wife: "Sometime the hating has to stop."[85]

The story of Eric Lomax illustrates many features of forgiveness, helps correct misconceptions, and answers some of our fears regarding forgiving others.

First, forgiveness is a process that takes time. Forgiveness cannot be rushed, pushed, or pleaded for. Take your time; face and accept the emotions you feel; decide what you will and won't accept; allow time for yourself to heal. In the beginning, you may find it impossible to forgive, but after much time, perhaps what was unthinkable becomes a reality—an enemy becomes a friend. At some point, you may choose to forgive. When you are ready, forgiveness can provide an alternative to pain, anxiety, anger, stress, feelings of resentment, depression, or desires for revenge. Forgiveness is not something an offender can demand, nor something a church authority can impose, nor even something that you must do. But you can open yourself to a process of forgiveness—one that will take time. Forgiveness can be given, but it can also require certain changes or boundaries before it is granted. Reconciliation may even happen, and the relationship may be even stronger, but this outcome is distinct from forgiveness. In other words, in some situations you can genuinely forgive and yet still have substantial boundaries in place that limit further interactions.

Second, forgiveness is hard, but it can be made much easier by the remorse and evident change of the perpetrator. Forgiveness is much more difficult when the offender thinks they have done nothing wrong. It can also be made easier by the imaginative "examined life" that places yourself in the position of the one who has harmed you.

Third, forgiveness is not forgetting. Forgiveness is not a mental switch where we try to switch off and forget everything, a mental game where we are always on the losing side. In fact, we must remember in order to forgive. To forgive, we need to count the cost and recognize the damage. Forgiveness is acknowledging the actual harm that people do. We should not say "Hey, it is no big deal" when it is. Forgiveness does not downplay, excuse, or ignore the harm done.

Fourth, forgiveness releases the person's hold over you. Many studies have shown the physical and mental health benefits of forgiveness—including reduced stress levels and stronger immune systems.[86] Forgiveness can release us from depression, feelings of resentment, or anxiety. Our fear is that if we forgive, this person will then take advantage of us, abuse us further, or control our lives. In fact, forgiveness releases us from bitterness, anger, or desires for revenge. It releases us from the person's past behavior that still controls our present and future. With forgiveness, we resist becoming like the people who have harmed us, for we no longer seek to do to them what they did to us.

Fifth, and finally, forgiveness offers hope. Forgiveness is an offer of kindness—to yourself and to the other person. Forgiveness is kind to you, for it frees you from being controlled by the other person's behavior. It is kind to the other person, for it offers them an opportunity for change. Forgiveness can stop the cycle of evil by not adding to the harm done and can lead to further empathy and understanding for those who have hurt us. Forgiveness releases us from bondage to other people's behavior and offers hope to the offender, and to others, that life can be better and worth living.

Chapter 3

Stories and Games: A Fun Life

> The universe is made of stories, not of atoms.
> —Muriel Rukeyser

> If you want your children to be intelligent,
> read them fairy tales.
> —Albert Einstein

> All reality is a game.
> —Iain Banks

So far, we have covered what I consider to be essential building blocks in the quest for the good and worthwhile life—such as disruption, the examined life, relational failure, repentance, and forgiveness. To move our conversation forward, we'll now consider assembling these blocks and others into a more cohesive structure. This chapter places these building blocks within two larger explanatory frameworks that further help us with the questions: What type of life is worth living? In seeking the good life, what should we change and why? What will inspire us to live well? And how does Christianity help or hinder this quest for the good life? I will connect these questions and others to the two broad rubrics of stories and games. Both provide larger contexts or frameworks for furthering our discussion.

For the life worth living, we need, among other things, direction, inspiration, hope, meaning, purpose, goals, and wisdom. I will argue that where these come from depends on the stories we tell and the games we play. We all have stories and we all play games, so it is essential that we tell excellent stories and play games well, because they influence the persons we are and what we aspire to be. For the life worth living, we need good stories and good games. Christianity itself rises and falls based on the games it plays and the stories it tells.

The subtitle for this chapter, "A Fun Life," is meant in the sense that the best stories and games are fun—a source of pleasure and play, but this life is not without its challenges and difficulties. We will first consider game theory and then move to storytelling.

The games we play

When the mathematical genius John von Neumann (1903–57) sat down to figure out how he could use mathematics to improve his poker playing, little did he realize the repercussions of his inquiry, not only in mathematics but also in almost every other field of inquiry. Considered the father of game theory, Neumann, with the economist Oskar Morgenstern, produced the founding textbook, *Theory of Games and Economic Behavior*, that revolutionized economics.

When playing a game such as poker, you have limited information (you cannot see all the cards), other players will deceive you, and they intend to win. Game theory is about what decisions and strategies you should use to achieve a favorable outcome.

Games comprise three primary areas: players, strategies, and outcomes. A basic form of a game is a two-person game where a win for one player means a loss for the other. Known as a zero-sum game, the outcome of this type of game adds up to zero—a win (+1) is offset by the other player's loss (-1). These games are one hundred percent competitive with no cooperation between players.

In a positive-sum game, however, your win does not mean a total loss for your opponent and involves some cooperation and competition. In such games, all players benefit, the outcome being positive. The cliché "win-win situation" refers to a positive sum game where all players benefit from the outcome. Trade between two nations is a classic example of a positive-sum game.

Game theory started in mathematics, but expanded to other disciplines including psychology, economics, politics, evolutionary biology, warfare, and even theology. We can conceive of most, if not all, interactions between people in terms of a game: people bidding on an eBay auction, the Cuban missile crisis, a couple arguing with each other, a job applicant negotiating a salary, airlines overbooking flights on the assumption that some passengers will not turn up, the process to achieve tenure at a university, a film or music audition, a criminal taking a plea agreement instead of a jury trial, a person sacrificing their life for the sake of another.

The diverse ways we structure games have implications for relationships and the good life. A married couple may frame an argument as a zero-sum game where each one maneuvers, like chess pieces on a board, to achieve a winning position—a position that means a defeat for their partner. Christian or secular organizations may frame their institutional identity as zero-sum games. Rules and beliefs establish and dictate how and why the game is played and who may play it. If you play, you play to win. If you play, you may only play if you stick to the parochial system; otherwise you are out. In these zero-sum games, a community builds a petty game with rules and beliefs that exclude a multitude of other realities, creating a system of thought that is placed above people—especially outsiders. There will be little flourishing of humankind with a zero-sum mentality that demands winners and losers.

The prisoner's dilemma: defect or cooperate?

The most famous example in game theory is the prisoner's dilemma, devised by Merrill Flood and Melvin Dresher. The basic idea of the prisoner's dilemma is this: The police have arrested you and a partner-in-crime on suspicion of robbing a bank. Lucky for you, the prosecutor lacks enough evidence to convict. You and your friend, however, are locked in separate, isolated cells and the prosecutor comes to you with a few options:

- Confess and we will let you go free and put your friend behind bars for fifteen years.
- Don't confess and if your partner confesses, we will put you in jail for fifteen years.
- If you both confess, we will drop the penalty to three years.
- If neither of you talk, well, we have enough evidence to convict you on a lesser charge and put you both away for six months.

What do you do? The dilemma is this: the rational choice is to confess, no matter what your friend does. If your friend does not confess, you go free. If your friend confesses, you only get three years instead of fifteen. But here is the catch: if you both keep silent the jail time is even less—only six months instead of three years. Do you confess or stay silent, or in the language of game theory, do you defect or cooperate? In the prisoner's dilemma, the rational choice is to defect, but the best potential outcome for both of you is to cooperate and keep silent.

Cooperation needs a relational connection. To achieve the best outcome, we need trust, but trust is vulnerable to exploitation. Do you trust your friend enough, because if you both cooperate, you have gamed the system and only receive a six-month sentence? Here, game theory underscores that trust and cooperation achieves the best outcome for everyone. The rational choice is not always ideal. The relational choice is the best.

Game theorists have studied many variations of the prisoner's dilemma, including iterative cases. Most interactions in life are not one-off. Instead of a one-off game, what happens when we repeat the game a hundred times? What strategy should we now adopt? The answer was discovered in two experiments organized by the political scientist Robert Axelrod, author of the highly influential *The Evolution of Cooperation*, a book that opened with the question: "Under what conditions will cooperation emerge in a world of egoists without central authority?"[87] Axelrod invited game theorists in economics, psychology, sociology, evolutionary biology, political science, mathematics, physics, and computer science to submit computer programs that would compete against each other in an iterative prisoner's dilemma scenario. What program would receive the highest score? One that was more willing to cooperate? One that defected all the time?

Axelrod describes some of the programs:[88]

Massive Retaliatory Strike: Cooperate at first, but after a defection from an opponent, retaliate for the rest of the game.

Tester: This program tries to find out what you are like, so it attacks in the first move. If met with retaliation, it will cooperate for a while. Then it will defect again, just to see how much it can get away with.

Jesus: Always cooperate.

Lucifer: Always defect.

If Tester plays Massive retaliatory strike, they both do poorly. Tester defects on the first move and Massive Retaliatory Strike defects from then on.

If Lucifer plays Jesus, Lucifer wins.

Axelrod thought that the winning program would contain thousands or tens of thousands of lines of code. The mathematical psychologist Anatol Rapoport submitted the highest-scoring program, and it was also one of the simplest, five lines of code, a tit-for-tat program, where cooperation was met with cooperation, and defection met with defection. Overall, the top-ranking programs were all nice, and on average, the defector programs scored significantly lower.

Axelrod described the tit-for-tat program as nice, retaliatory, forgiving, and clear. The program is nice, because it starts with cooperation. (Or if the word "nice" appears too weak, substitute "kind.") It retaliates to discourage the other player from continued defection. It forgives and quickly restores cooperation. It is clear because it is not duplicitous. Its actions are straightforward and easily interpreted, thus providing a basis for long-term cooperation. The one distinguishing feature of programs that did well, versus those that did poorly, was being nice. In other words, start with trust and cooperation, and avoid unnecessary conflict. A nice player is never the first to defect and cooperates whenever the other player cooperates. Surprisingly, nice people finish first.

Tit-for-tat is the most successful strategy when the prisoner's dilemma is played many times. You start with cooperation and basic trust. If the other player cooperates, you continue to cooperate. If they defect, then you respond with defection. The strategy punishes those who take advantage of other players' trust and generosity. The strategy, however, also allows for a change of mind. After deflecting, your opponent may once again decide to cooperate with you. In tit-for-tat, you respond with cooperation.

To express these ideas in more theological language, for an iterative game that achieves the best outcomes for all players, we need trust, forgiveness, and repentance. Trust is necessary for cooperation, and as we cooperate, we repeatedly send the message that we are trustworthy. In a repeated game, however, there will be failures by all players. Forgiveness is necessary, for it allows us to continue to play the game when a defector decides to cooperate. Repentance is necessary, for it allows us to change from defecting to cooperating. It turns out that forgiveness and repentance are even more important than first realized by game theorists. In the complicated world of relationships, people can misinterpret signals. Perhaps a player intended to cooperate, but her actions are misconstrued as a defection. A player can make a mistake, or perhaps they just need a second chance. Does the game now have to continue with repeated retaliation? Here is where a small tweak optimizes the tit-for-tat program; named "generous tit-for-tat," it will randomly throw in a forgiveness about ten percent of the time. Call it an undeserved kindness that breaks a cycle of repeated defection.

Playing games that benefit all players depends on healthy relationships. If we are in an agreeable relationship with other players, we are more likely to cooperate than defect. These relationships encourage a willingness to forgive and repent. Relationships temper our fear that we will be tricked, and relationships temper our greed that seeks outcomes advantageous to us while at the expense of other players.

The tit-for-tat strategy illustrates that a relational approach is far from being a pathetic pushover. Unconditional pacifism is a losing strategy because psychopaths and con artists are always scouting to exploit some unwary soul, softie, or sucker. A relational approach that includes trust, forgiveness, and repentance also includes a credible threat of repercussion for defection. "If another person sins, rebuke that person; if there is repentance, forgive" (Luke 17:3). A relational approach will retaliate, for example, against the zero-sum games of patriarchy, racism, and other forms of prejudice. It starts with trust and cooperation, is quick to forgive, but will also punish defectors.

There is, however, a problem with a game repeated a finite amount of times. If you know the game is finite and is going to end after a hundred moves, then even after repeated cooperation, the reasonable strategy is to defect in the last move. Take the money and run—there can be no retaliation because the game has ended. This suggests the importance of infinite games, games that continue indefinitely, where there is no end and therefore no temptation to defect at the end.

Infinite games

The religious scholar James Carse has developed this idea in *Finite and Infinite Games: A Vision of Life as Play and Possibility*. Carse distinguishes between two types of games: finite and infinite. There are substantial differences between the characteristics and goals of finite and infinite games. Carse writes, "A finite game is played for the purpose of winning, an infinite game for the purpose of continuing the play."[89] A finite game ends when somebody wins; thus finite games need fixed boundaries and unchanging rules to decide who wins. In contrast, infinite games are ongoing and have no fixed boundaries or rules.

Finite games are defined by their boundaries, whereas infinite games are defined by their horizon. Boundaries are fixed and clear, and one cannot move beyond a boundary. But in an infinite game the horizon is open-ended—it is a direction that we move toward, a place we never reach, a journey always open to newness and surprise.

For Carse, the goal of players of finite games is to become powerful, entitled Master Players, supremely competent in every detail of the game that they play as if the game is already finished. And because a finite game always ends, finite players must repeatedly play to prove they are winners.

One characteristic of an infinite game is that there are no winners or losers because the game always continues. In a finite game, the last thing you want is surprise, whereas in an infinite game, surprise is one reason for continuing to play. An infinite game is fluid and open ended, and the reasons for playing an infinite game are not to become powerful or to win. The concern of infinite players is "not with power but with vision."[90]

Those who play bounded and finite games are undoubtedly threatened by infinite games, which they perceive to be exclusive and devastating to their games.

Consider the example of apartheid: "What—you want to give blacks the vote? That is excluding our exclusive views!" The finite, zero-sum game of apartheid resulted in a loss for most of the population of South Africa, but racists were eventually rebuked. Racists were invited, however, into a different game where their rules of exclusion were not part of the play.

Or consider again the example of Christianity. Christianity has often been a finite game, but in the quest to promote the good life, it can be conceived as an infinite game. We would be incredibly naïve to assume that there is just one message of Christianity. In the church's two-thousand-year history, people have expressed a multitude of different ideas about Jesus and offered countless different versions of Christianity.

Here is Christianity formulated as a finite, zero-sum game: Christians win; everyone else loses. Christians are master players, essential to this grand game, a game that has a definitive conclusion resulting in a win for us, and a loss for everyone else. The game is one of good versus evil, us versus them. Our particular beliefs and rules establish fixed boundaries of the game and distinguish us from non-Christians (and even other Christians) and their games. You may join and play, but only if you accept the rules that structure and direct our game. The benefits include power, titles, solid explanations, fixed boundaries, solidarity with us, and a winning hand.

As a finite, zero-sum game Christianity has had little difficulty aligning itself with patriarchy, slavery, racism, antisemitism, anti-LBGTQ, hate crimes, torture and death for infidels, and colluding with empires—Roman, Spanish, British, and American. In each case, there are clear winners and losers. If Christianity is set up as a megalomaniacal finite game, it is impossible to play an infinite game. By its nature, it excludes the possibility of Christianity as an infinite game.

Here is an example of Christianity formulated as an infinite game: In the beginning was the game maker, and the one who plays, and the one who invites others to join the game and continue the play. Jesus plays fast and loose with the rules, dissolves boundaries and fixed beliefs, and opens new horizons of possibility. In an infinite game, the central themes of the

Christian story—incarnation, life, death, resurrection—are articulated in ways that place people and relationships above the system. There are no winners or losers—there is neither Jew nor gentile, slave nor free, male nor female (Gal 3:28). Jesus is not a master player but an infinite player who invites all to an infinite game by including the excluded and rebuking the excluders. Anyone can play, no titles are awarded, no winners are announced, and boundaries are replaced by an infinite horizon.

This infinite game is characterized by vision and openness, where beliefs and rules are continually rewritten in order to keep the game going. In an infinite game, there is no end of play, and if necessary, infinite players will choose death over life for this type of game to continue.

Christianity conceived as an infinite game thus places stories far above religious beliefs. Religious beliefs are certain, bounded, and are not the visionary story. Rather, religious beliefs are small chips knocked out of the narrative structure. Whereas beliefs often end the conversation, a story invites further discovery, directs people to the horizon, continues the game, and reformulates the conversation. Stories have development, surprises, twists, paradoxes, and uncertainties. And it is to stories that we now turn.

The stories we tell

Once upon a time, there was a great king . . .

In the 1850s archeologists, excavating the royal library at Nineveh, made one of the most sensational archeological finds ever. The library had belonged to Ashurbanipal, an Assyrian king who was famous for his military exploits (defeating Egypt and Elam) and his scholarly proclivities (collecting writings throughout Mesopotamia). Ashurbanipal had amassed a remarkable collection of tens of thousands of cuneiform tablets that he housed in the library at Nineveh—the greatest city of the time. Ashurbanipal died in 627 BCE, and in 612 BCE a combined army that included Babylonians and Persians destroyed Nineveh. They razed and burned the city—perhaps inadvertently baking the tablets and thus preserving them for posterity. The tablets had not seen the light of day for over two thousand years.

Among the thousands of tablets sent back to the British Museum were a group of twelve tablets that lay in the museum for another nineteen years until a self-taught scholar, George Smith (1840–76), translated from Akkadian the eleventh tablet, and to his astonishment read a story of a great flood—a story that predated, from the earliest Sumerian sources, the Bible's account of Noah by at least a thousand years. He jumped up and rushed around the room. And rumor says that in his excitement he tore off some of his clothes. Smith was reading what we now know as the Epic of Gilgamesh—one of the oldest works of literature.

In 1872, Smith cemented his fame when he delivered a reading on the eleventh tablet to the Society of Biblical Archeology, which included a mass of reporters and even Prime Minister William Gladstone in attendance. Tragically, when Smith went back to Nineveh to do further excavation, he fell sick with dysentery and died, only thirty-six years old.

The Epic of Gilgamesh that Smith uncovered tells the story of Gilgamesh, a king of the great city Uruk, a Homer-like hero with divine parentage. He is two parts god and one part human. And like the Homeric epics, this story has an odyssey and a search for everlasting fame.

The first half of the story develops the relationship between Gilgamesh and his close friend Enkidu, and together they accomplish some great deeds. They kill the guardian of the cedar forest—the monster Humbaba—and the bull from heaven who was sent from the goddess Ishtar. But in their quest for reputation and glory, their actions are their undoing. After they kill Humbaba and the bull from heaven, the gods take Enkidu's life.

In the second part of the epic, the death of Enkidu spurs Gilgamesh on a quest for everlasting life and to find the one man, Utanapishtim, whom the gods made immortal after the great flood. Gilgamesh's quest is no longer for fame and glory, but now a search for eternal life—to find the only man who became immortal and to learn from him the secret of eternal life.

This journey takes Gilgamesh to the netherworld, to the mountain into which the sun sets at nightfall, whose foundations reach to the underworld and that is guarded by man-scorpions. After entering this mountain, with the aid of a ferryman, Gilgamesh crosses the waters of death that separate an Edenic garden from where Utanapishtim lives forever.

When he finally reaches Utanapishtim, he gets to ask the one question on his mind: "How may I find the life that I am seeking?" The answer Gilgamesh gets is that nothing endures, every person dies, every building collapses, every contract doesn't last, even master and slave are the same in death. But if this is the case, Gilgamesh asks, how is it that Utanapishtim has entered the company of the gods? Utanapishtim then tells the story of the great flood. People were making so much noise and disturbing the sleep of the gods that the gods exterminated the lot. Utanapishtim was warned in a dream to tear down his house and build a boat. He filled the boat with his family, riches, and the artisans who helped him, as well as tame and wild beasts. With the approaching storm, he entered the boat, and the gods unleashed the flood for six days and nights, such a conflagration that it even terrified these same gods. After the boat settled on a mountain,

Utanapishtim first sent out a dove, then a swallow, and then a raven to confirm that dry land had appeared. He then sacrificed to the gods, and the god Enlil rewarded Utanapishtim with immortality. But now he must live apart from the gods and mortals.

Gilgamesh leaves to return home with another quest to find an underwater plant that can restore youth. He recovers the plant, but a snake steals it from him. The snake then eats the plant, loses its skin, and becomes young again—an etiological myth on why snakes lose their skins. Gilgamesh at last returns to Uruk, but without everlasting life and without the plant to restore his youth, he dies. A central message of this ancient story is that we will never find eternal life. Only the gods live forever.

As far back as we have written records, we find that humans are storytellers. From the earliest writings, humans have used stories to figure out their world and to help explain what it means to be human. In fact, we could define humans as storytellers. It is our distinguishing, wonderful characteristic. From the Epic of Gilgamesh to Homer to Harry Potter, we use stories to ask questions and to explore our humanity: Is immortality to be found? What does it mean to live a good life? What is worth pursuing? What might be our undoing? How should we live in the face of our mortality? What is real and true? We turn to stories for answers.

Quests to the underworld, accounts of gods, heroines, and heroes, monsters and snakes, all make for grand stories. But they are attempts to understand ourselves and our world. Even the monsters say something about us, such as Godzilla arising from the use of nuclear weapons. Monsters have always occupied the fringes of knowledge. The old cartographers illustrated the as-yet-unexplored parts of their maps with all kinds of fanciful creatures, mostly scary. And when we ran out of monsters here on terra firma, we found aliens in outer space.

Stories help us discover what we value. Stories help humanity survive and thrive, and they create and join communities together. A community is a group that has shared stories. Stories allow us to reimagine ourselves—to flitter between the imaginary world and our own. We can imagine ourselves in the story and question how would we act under similar circumstances. What characters would we like to be? Steven Pinker notes that one catalyst for the decline in violence was the rise in book publication and the reading of fiction.[91] Thus, stories can also encourage empathy and bring transformation.

A story is not life itself, but a dialogue with life. A cohesive narrative explains some part of our humanity, what we are, what we aspire to be, and what we could be under similar circumstances. Given this, we should be highly aware of the quality of stories that we are consuming. There are most probably good evolutionary advantages to telling, hearing, and buying into an excellent story. And these stories—the fittest stories—are the ones that survive and can continue to survive by developing and adapting to their environment.

Stories of science

Who are the revered storytellers? At one time it was the theologians, and religion supplied all the answers. Around the nineteenth century it was musicians and artists, and we have the representative figure of Franz Liszt claiming to be the new prophet bringing revelation. The philosophers Nietzsche and Heidegger agreed—the artists are the ones who have the truth and not scientists. This wasn't to last, and the decline of music and art in modern education is disheartening and limits our resources to pursue the good life. Prophets come and go, and today our esteemed storytellers are scientists with their remarkable stories.

Some of the most successful and inspiring stories today are told by science. At first glance, it may seem that the scientific enterprise has little to do with narratives. Of course, scientific stories are different narratives from those told by poets, musicians, novelists, artists, filmmakers, and the religious. Yet scientific theories have successful and compelling narratives that, by using various tools and models, have opened new vistas on the universe. In the twenty-first century there are many wonderful narratives told by cosmology, geology, paleontology, biology, genetics, and many others.

Caltech physicist Sean Carroll connects science and story:

> We tell stories about how the universe works, but we don't simply tell any old stories that come to mind; we are dramatically constrained by experimental data and by consistency with the basic principles we think we do understand. Those constraints are enormously powerful—enough that we can sit at our desks, thinking hard, extending our ideas way beyond anything we've directly experienced, and come up with good ideas about how things really work. Most such ideas don't turn out to be right—that's science for you—but some of them do.[92]

For our purposes, I'll summarize two scientific stories as examples among many that we could choose.[93] We will then consider the significance of scientific stories for this quest for the worthwhile life.

Geology

The science of modern geology traces back to the work of James Hutton (1726–97), one of the first to discover evidence for the immense age of the earth. Hutton has been called "the man who found time."[94] Prior to Hutton, most people thought the earth was comparatively young—measured in thousands of years. Studying layers of sedimentary rock on the coast of Scotland led Hutton to one of the most remarkable conclusions in all of science. He reasoned that these sedimentary layers resulted from a repeating process: rivers erode the land and deposit layers of silt in the sea. Over time, these layers are buried, compressed, and then eventually turn to rock. Geological forces eventually lifted the rocks out of the sea and the entire process starts again.

The question naturally arose: How long had all this taken? Hutton's conclusion was that the earth was ancient beyond imagining. It was "unknowably old."[95] Hutton had discovered geological time. Stephen Jay Gould wrote of Hutton: "He burst the boundaries of time, thereby establishing geology's most distinctive and transforming contribution to human thought—Deep Time."[96] Hutton didn't provide an estimate for the age of the earth because there was no available method or apparatus to help him. Today, with radiometric dating, we can date accurately various rocks such as meteorites that put our earth and solar system at about 4.67 billion years old.

In August 2014, my family and I had the incredible experience of hiking in the Grand Canyon. On one hike, we started at the top of the canyon and walked the seven-mile South Kaibab Trail to the Colorado River. The hike covers one vertical mile descent of rock—igneous, sedimentary, and metamorphic—that spans 1.8 billion years, a stunning visual timeline of earth's history unmatched anywhere in the world. Every vertical meter of rock covers a million years. At the top of the canyon we were standing on what remains of an ancient inland sea. The rocks are about 250 million years old and contain many marine fossils, such as corals, sponges, brachiopods, and crinoids. This is analogous to the rocks near the top of Mount Everest that contain fossilized seashells. The summit of Everest is marine limestone and once was an ocean floor. This surprising fact is explained by plate tectonics, now an established theory, although only dating back to the 1960s. Continents, moving about as fast as toenails grow, over millions of years, have transformed the earth and raised mountains from the seabed.

Progressing further down the canyon, at around 280 million years, they have discovered fossils of eight-inch-wingspan dragonflies. At 525 million years, we find many people's favorite—trilobites. As you go down, each layer of sedimentary rock tells a story of the ancient landscapes of northern

Arizona—from a shallow sea like the Caribbean, to a vast desert like the Sahara, together with tracks from reptiles, scorpions, and spiders. The Grand Canyon is a remarkable story in rock that has taken considerable scientific expertise, investigation, and research to be told.

Evolutionary theory

Evolutionary theory is another scientific story that lays claim to the "greatest story ever told." Evolution had been proposed before Charles Darwin, from ancient Greek philosophers to one of the great eighteenth-century intellectuals, Erasmus Darwin (Charles's grandfather), in his work *Zoonomia* (1794–96), to Darwin's contemporary Alfred Wallace who independently discovered the theory of evolution through natural selection. Charles Darwin, however, is rightly given central place in the establishment of the theory of evolution. Darwin's theory finds its origin in his almost-five-year voyage around the world on the HMS Beagle, a remarkable journey that Darwin regarded as the most influential event in his life. His book *The Voyage of the Beagle* (1845) documents his travels and observations, and is still worth reading today as one of the great travel journals.

Some twenty-three years after his return Darwin published his *On the Origin of Species* (1859), laying out the theory that living organisms evolved from a common ancestor through a process he called natural selection. This process starts with the struggle for existence—there is always limited food and other resources, and organisms usually produce more offspring than can survive. In a particular environment (or change of environment), organisms may inherit traits that give them a better chance to survive and reproduce, whereas organisms with deleterious traits die out. Over time, these changes add up until the species differs from its ancestor. This is evolution by natural selection. Darwin left out a discussion on humankind in *On the Origin of Species*, but he tackled this topic later in his other famous work, *The Descent of Man, and Selection in Relation to Sex* (1871), where he argued for the evolution of humankind and for his theory of sexual selection—how many behaviors and anatomical features arise through competition for mates, such as bright plumage to impress mates or horns to fight rivals.

Darwin's theory has secured its place as one of the greatest scientific theories of all time. It is hard to underestimate its importance for a multitude of scientific disciplines. Since Darwin first planted the seed, evidence for evolution has grown and flowered far beyond what he had at his disposal and what he could have imagined.

By the middle of the twentieth century, evolutionary theory had developed into the neo-Darwinian synthesis. Part of this synthesis was the joining of Darwin's theory to genetic discoveries, which trace to the work of Gregor Mendel (1822–84)—that DNA held the secret of how inherited traits, including mutations, are passed to descendants. Darwin lacked the benefit of knowing the laws of heredity and the existence of DNA. Now, through an analysis of DNA, we can trace our evolutionary relationships to other living organisms: from our closest living relative, the chimpanzee (with whom we share around 98.7 percent identical DNA), through dogs, mice, flies, and worms. By comparing the genomes of distinct species and based on similarities of DNA, we can now construct an evolutionary tree of life—a tree that is remarkably like the fossil record.

Evolutionary theory has continued to undergo considerable development from Darwin's original theory, through the neo-Darwinian synthesis, to the new science of evolutionary development, known informally as "Evo Devo." Evo Devo can now explain how different animal forms come about, how large-scale changes in animal design arise. Sean Carroll, a biologist at the forefront of Evo Devo research, in his *Endless Forms Most Beautiful: The New Science of Evo Devo*, explains that Evo Devo started with the unexpected discovery that particular genes in fruit flies that govern their body design had exact counterparts in other animals, including worms, mice, and humans.[97] Through the discovery of master regulatory or developmental genes, such as the *Hox* or *Pax-6* genes, biologists can now explain how widely different species use the same genetic building blocks to evolve different shapes, body parts, and larger forms. Remarkably, macro changes in design are made using the same tools—a genetic tool kit in place over five hundred million years ago—with just a few changes in genetic switches.[98]

Evolution, like any delightful story, has its twists and turns, villains and victims, dead ends and fruitful avenues. There is conflict, drama, tragedy, hope, life, death, sex, and surprising developments. Surprises such as the Permian extinction (250 million years ago and the largest extinction ever) or the Cretaceous-Tertiary extinction of the dinosaurs (65 million years ago) interrupt the normal flow of the story. These catastrophes, however, set in motion remarkable developments, such as the rise of mammals after the dinosaur extinction—and one path leading to *Homo sapiens* with even more surprising developments, such as the emergence of consciousness, language, the capability for abstract thought, and the ability to tell stories.

* * *

The stories of modern science rank among the brilliant achievements of humankind. And irrespective of the gripes from some, almost everyone accepts modern science in their everyday life—from flying in planes, to using computers and smartphones, to sentencing someone based on DNA evidence, to modern medicine.

People accept modern science because it works. Astrophysicist Neil Degrass Tyson has quipped, "The good thing about Science is that it's true, whether or not you believe in it."[99] That's funny but it conceals an important feature of science—that what science considers as true has changed over time. Of course, the findings of science stand irrespective of our personal beliefs. Quantum field theory stands, even though Einstein disliked the idea. Science at the beginning of the twenty-first century is, however, remarkably different from science at the beginning of the twentieth century. Consider something as fundamental as water. Is our conception of H_2O ever likely to change? Will water always be two atoms of Hydrogen and one atom of Oxygen? Generally speaking, yes. But since 1932 we have been able to create heavy water—where the hydrogen nucleus not only contains a proton (as in normal hydrogen) but also a neutron. Furthermore, what we mean by "atom" differs from what we meant by it a hundred years ago. We use the same words—"atom," "molecule," "earth," "universe"—but the meanings have undergone profound changes. Our conception of what is real has changed. Thus, science has developed and sometimes significantly changed the stories it tells.

Most scientists are careful to qualify that they do not have the inviolable "Truth" and that they have not "proved" anything. Everything is open to new evidence and rational investigation. In 1900, when Lord Kelvin proclaimed that everything in physics had been discovered, except for a couple of clouds on the horizon—it wasn't long before the two clouds of relativity and quantum mechanics developed into massive hurricanes, disrupting the scientific community, and becoming new stories themselves. Physicists are unlikely to make Kelvin's flub again.

A few scientists even question the direction of some scientific stories. Two examples: string theory and the multiverse. Questions arise whether these theories will ever be empirically verified, whether they are worth pursuing, and whether modern physics has wandered into territory with grand mathematical theories that have little to no empirical evidence. But as Columbia physicist Brian Greene explains in *The Hidden Reality: Parallel Universes and the Deep Laws of the Cosmos*, the multiverse theory is not something physicists dreamed up for their own amusement; it arose from no less than nine separate fields in physics. These fields lead to the incredible conception of more universes than there are particles in our universe, where there is every possible version of you, including you with a prehensile tail.[100] We now have a story of infinite stories.

The other example, string theory, hopes to resolve the incompatibilities between the theories of relativity and quantum mechanics and provide a new unified theory. The theory holds that the smallest parts of matter are not atoms, electrons, or quarks, but one-dimensional loops of vibrating strings. The distinct vibrations of these strings give rise to all other particles. The theory also postulates that space has other hidden dimensions, hiding or curled up in our common three dimensions. String theory, if true, would have within its story the delightful implication that at the very smallest level of reality there is *music*—the vibration of strings.

Some scientific stories will achieve extraordinary success; others will fail. Errors and fraud will occur. Scientists are also human, so they are just as susceptible to human failings and foibles as everyone else, but in their favor, they have cooperation, repeatability, and accountability. An often-quoted remark by the statistician George Box, "All models are wrong, but some are useful," seems too clear-cut.[101] Some models are wrong. All models are provisional. Some models get better over time. Some models are highly probable. Some models are extremely useful, but even the best scientific models have fuzziness, tradeoffs, abstractions, generalizations, reductionism, approximations, and simplifications.

The conclusions of science even show that science will never arrive at all truth. We have Heisenberg's uncertainty principle that we can never simultaneously know the position and momentum of fundamental particles. We have Gödel's theorem—a mathematical proof that proves that we cannot prove everything by mathematics. In addition, the great distances in our known universe are limited by the speed of light. It would take one hundred thousand years just to traverse our galaxy at light speed. And if the universe keeps expanding, there will be galaxies forever beyond our sight, reach, and knowledge (never mind other possible universes). In fact, because of this expansion, if we left today traveling at the speed of light, only about 3 percent of the total number of galaxies would be reachable.[102]

Even given the remarkably successful stories of science, they don't answer all the questions we have. For human flourishing we need more stories than the ones that science tells. The story of evolution can, for example, uncover the development of morality in our species, but in the end cannot decide right from wrong. From the evolutionary story, do we stress cooperation or competition? Humans are implicated in the eradication of megafauna and other hominids, but this sordid evolutionary history serves as an example of how we ought not to live. The recent discovery that we share some Neanderthal DNA changes the story somewhat, in that we now know that *Homo sapiens* interbred with Neanderthals. But perhaps we still wiped them out. All is fair in love and war.

Science can explain how morality evolved to ensure a community's survival. Just as in order to survive we must respect the laws of gravity and not jump off tall buildings, functioning communities have a prohibition against murder. Science, broadly understood, can also help in deciding what is moral. We saw in game theory that cooperation is much better than winner-takes-all; that cooperation and trust are essential components for good relationships. And as our tools and data become better, we can discover what works better—what produces better relationships between people and societies. But this can only take us so far, and most scientists don't adopt scientism—the view that science can encompass all human thought, meaning, and experience.

There is an often-debated point: are there different ways of knowing? Does science have one way of knowing and religion another? Considering the two scientific stories above—geology and evolutionary theory—religion has repeatedly failed to discover what is true about the world. Despite these failures, some religious people still disparage these and other scientific disciplines. Nevertheless, we need more than what science can tell us, a point undisputed by most scientists. We need other stories that can direct, motivate, and provide value. Is this a particular kind of knowledge? The knowledge of what is just and unjust. The knowledge of what type of people we aspire to be. The knowledge of being profoundly moved by a piece of music or work of art. The knowledge of what choice to make. Part of the problem is how broadly we define "ways of knowing" or "knowledge."

There is no lab experiment to show the right choice among many. Scientific stories cannot capture all human experience. You don't have to be an ardent dualist to say that seeing and smelling a red rose is not entirely grasped by science. We could look at a lover's response to a red rose as a response to a particular wavelength of light, that the color red doesn't actually exist, that if we were a different species with different capabilities, we would see a different color or no color at all, and if we were vultures we wouldn't go around sniffing roses. But this is insufficient for a poet or lover. A pianist, deeply moved by playing Liszt's *B minor Sonata*, is not thinking of the intensity of the sound waves, the frequencies, the air compression, and how her ear is converting that air compression into impulses and sending them to her brain.

If people want to limit "ways of knowing" to science and the success of scientific methods to discover what is true about our universe, then we can talk about "ways of living." The poet, philosopher, artist, musician, or writer can be involved in endeavors that explore our humanity—finding ways of conceiving love and justice, ways of learning about ourselves and our relationships, ways of inspiring the life worth living. We have a big universe, however, with enough room for both science and the humanities to develop stories to correct, reorient, challenge, and inspire us.

This is no segue, however, to set up religions, and Christianity in particular, as the inspired source and direction of what is the just and good life. Christian stories have not provided a clear moral compass either in practice or in theory. Even in "ways of living" churches have often led in precisely the wrong direction. Large sections of the church still deny women all the rights given to men. Considering any ethical issue facing us in the twenty-first century, the stories that Christians tell are diverse, sometimes contradictory, and have no united clarion call. What follows will further illustrate the stories we tell—in particular, the storied nature of Christianity. Christians are storytellers, and in keeping with our overall dialog with Christianity, we will now look at some examples of the myriad stories that Christians tell.

Bible stories

The Bible is a compilation of stories. Some stories are based upon historical facts, many are not. Many of the stories are retellings or derivations from older sources. We know this from a multitude of evidence across various disciplines—from scientific disciplines to biblical studies. All converge and conclude this.

Take, for example, the first few books in the Hebrew Bible. There we have the accounts of creation in six days, the creation of the first two humans—Adam and Eve, the story of Noah and the worldwide flood, the Tower of Babel, the Exodus, and the conquest of Canaan.

Against this we have the evidence-based theories of modern cosmology, paleontology, archeology, genetics, evolutionary biology, geology, linguistics, and anthropology. We know from cosmology that the universe wasn't created in six days. We know from modern genetics that there were never just two people in the human population—that our population numbers were never less than a few thousand people, most probably around ten thousand people. In any event, in the line of species, there are never sharp breaks like that proposed with Adam and Eve. We know from evolutionary theory that humans are descendants of prior species going back to fish and beyond. We know from geology that there was never a worldwide flood, and from linguistics that languages did not develop in the way recounted in the story of Babel. And we know from archeology that there is scant evidence for the events describing the Exodus and conquest of Canaan. These events did not happen in the manner described in the Bible.

Multiple scientific fields provide a convergence of evidence showing beyond reasonable doubt that what we have here are ancient stories that are fiction. With the stories of science, we can now be reasonably sure of this. None of this is controversial to specialists in these fields. In addition, sometimes people who had a stake in these Bible stories established this evidence. For example, devout Christians first refuted the notion of a worldwide flood. Christian geologists rejected Flood geology (even before Darwin's theory appeared) based on evidence they uncovered.[103] As another example, Israeli archeologists were among those who established the Exodus and conquest narratives to be almost certainly fictional stories.[104]

For our examples of Bible stories, we will look at: (1) the Gospel of Matthew and (2) the stories that are told about the central figure of Christianity, Jesus of Nazareth.

Matthew's Gospel

Matthew's Gospel was written by an educated, unknown author, decades after the death of Jesus. Only much later, in the second century CE, did scribes add the titles to Matthew's Gospel and the three other Gospels. Scholars place the writing of Matthew around 80–90 CE, so the author is writing some fifty years after the death of Jesus. The author, who we will still call Matthew for convenience, is not an eyewitness to the events he describes, is writing in a different country (perhaps Antioch), and writes in Greek—a different language from the Aramaic most probably spoken by Jesus and his disciples. Some of the evidence that the author is not Matthew the disciple is that Matthew's Gospel borrows some 93 percent of Mark's Gospel (and Mark is neither a disciple nor an eyewitness). It is highly unlikely a disciple of Jesus would need to borrow extensively from another source. In addition, even when describing the call or conversion of the disciple Matthew, this author uses Mark's Gospel as a source. When he speaks about "Matthew," the disciple of Jesus, the writer never says "me" but speaks in the third person.

The writer is not, however, just sitting down and making up everything from thin air. We know Matthew depended primarily on Mark's Gospel, possibly other documents, and an oral tradition handed down to him. Most New Testament scholars hold to a two-source hypothesis for Matthew. Scholars have long theorized that Matthew also had in his possession a collection of sayings, a document named Q, from the German word *Quelle*, meaning "source." This idea comes from a comparison of the Gospels of Luke and

Matthew. Luke also relied on Mark to write his Gospel, but there is material that is common to both Matthew and Luke that is not found in Mark. Scholars have labeled this material Q, which could be a lone source or a collection of documents. This theory, however, isn't ironclad and lacks physical evidence. We don't have in our possession this hypothetical document Q. There are other persuasive, simpler theories, such as that Matthew used Mark, and then subsequently Luke used both Mark and Matthew.

Out of the 661 verses in Mark, Matthew uses about 93 percent, and with no acknowledgment. Although Matthew borrowed most of Mark, he made substantial additions and corrections, and overall adapted the material for his Jewish audience. Matthew tries to "improve" Mark's vernacular Greek. Gone is Mark's "Messianic secret" theme and most of the ignorance and confusion of the disciples. There is no virgin birth story in Mark, and the original version of Mark ends abruptly at Mark 16:8 with the empty tomb. Matthew adds the nativity, extended resurrection, and ascension material.

In many places, Matthew corrected Mark for errors, or at the very least, corrected possible misunderstandings. A few examples:

1. Mark speaks of "in the days of Abiathar the high priest" (Mark 2:26). Matthew leaves this out (Matt 12:4), perhaps because he knew it should have been Ahimelech (1 Sam 21:1–6).

2. In Mark 5:1, Mark speaks of Gerasenes near a large body of water. Matthew changes this to Gadarenes (Matt 8:28). Gerasa is nowhere near the Sea of Galilee, whereas Gadara is much closer.

3. In Mark 7:31 there are two possible errors in geography—that Sidon is south of Tyre (when it is 22 miles to the north) and that the Sea of Galilee is in the midst of the Decapolis. Matthew simply removes these details (Matt 15:29).

4. In Mark 1:2–3, Mark quotes a passage from Malachi 3:1, but says that it is from the prophet Isaiah. In Matthew 3:3, Matthew drops the text not found in Isaiah. Very few ancient writers would have access to complete scrolls of individual books of the Hebrew Bible, and usually worked from a list of quotations based on various themes, such as were found at Qumran. Mark most probably had a list of quotations that were listed under the prophet Isaiah, but in his list the passage from Malachi was included and hence the mistake. Matthew makes a similar error in Matthew 27:9 when he writes about the death of Judas, misattributing a statement to Jeremiah that it is found in Zechariah.

Of course, those who hold to an inerrant or infallible Bible have their explanations (often long and pedantic) for these and many other discrepancies and errors. But they are not the obvious and simplest explanations. The New Testament scholar Bart Ehrman describes a turning point in his studies at Princeton Seminary. He had arrived as an evangelical and had submitted a paper on Mark chapter 2, giving a complicated argument why Mark was correct about Abiathar being the high priest when David ate the bread in the temple, when in fact it was Abiathar's father Ahimelech. His professor wrote a brief note at the end of the paper: "Maybe Mark just made a mistake."[105] Ehrman came to agree with his professor, an example of Occam's razor[106] at work—among competing explanations, the simpler theory is to be preferred.

Whether Matthew is correcting errors where Mark wasn't as familiar with Jewish customs and the geography of Palestine, or whether Matthew is simply clarifying material for his audience, what is clear is that Matthew gives no second thought to correcting or improving Mark in style or content.

When it comes to stories, however, on some occasions Matthew's adaptation of Mark results in a story that falls flat. For example, in Mark we find the tension-filled story where Jairus, a synagogue leader, frantically urges Jesus to come and heal his daughter, who is dying (Mark 5:21–43). But Jesus doesn't help Jairus's daughter right away. Instead, Jesus is insistent on discovering and exposing the woman who touched his cloak to be healed from her hemorrhages. After this delay, Jairus's daughter dies. In Matthew, however, the author drastically shortens the story so that the synagogue leader approaches Jesus with the news that his daughter has already died, which not only removes all the tension of Mark's narrative but assumes the unlikely scenario that a ruler of the synagogue would have at the outset thought that Jesus could raise people from the dead (Matt 9:18–26).

Overall, Matthew, while using Mark as a basis, wrote his Gospel for his Jewish audience to show that Jesus is the Messiah, the new Moses, and the new Israel. He writes not as a historian but as a theologian. His arrangement of the material and his emphasis on how Jesus is the fulfillment of the Hebrew Bible and what God promised, confirms that this is a theologically constructed text.

Dale C. Allison Jr. in *The New Moses: A Matthean Typology*[107] shows how Matthew describes Jesus as a recapitulation of Israel's history. Drawing from Allison we can list the ways Matthew arranges the life of Jesus to follow the history of Israel and to portray Jesus as the new Moses[108]:

- Patterned after Israel, Jesus is taken into Egypt and then returns to the Promised Land.

- Herod's killing of the infants parallels Pharaoh's call to kill infant Hebrew boys.
- Jesus' baptism follows the passing of the Israelites through the Red Sea.
- After his baptism, Jesus goes into the wilderness for forty days, patterned after the forty years the Israelites spent in the Sinai desert.
- There in the desert, Jesus is tempted, just as Israel was tempted for bread in the wilderness. As Israel was tempted to worship other gods, Jesus is tempted to worship Satan.
- After returning from the desert, Jesus calls the twelve disciples, patterned after the twelve tribes of Israel.
- Afterwards Jesus gives the Sermon on the Mount. Matthew, in making Jesus the new Moses, has Jesus giving the new law on a mountain. And like the giving of the law by Moses, the Sermon on the Mount has its own blessings and curses.
- Jesus does miracles and healing. Jesus feeds the multitudes as the Israelites were fed with manna in the desert. Jesus is a prophet "like unto Moses."
- The twelve disciples are then sent out to conquer the land like the events described in Joshua. Jesus was transfigured on the mountain like Moses, and while transfigured he speaks with Moses and Elijah who represent the law and the prophets.
- Finally, Jesus is handed over to the gentiles as Israel was handed over to the gentile nations.

To expand on just one example above, scholars have noted that the beginning of Matthew (chapters 1–2) is a rewriting of the Exodus story. Herod is the new Pharaoh. Like Pharaoh, Herod kills the young children. This account of Herod's slaughter of the infants is unique to Matthew. No other biblical writer mentions this event. In fact, no other ancient writer mentions this slaughter. It is unlikely that other writers, such as Philo or Josephus, who were extremely interested in and knowledgeable of Israel, would miss this incident. This story is understandable, however, when we consider Matthew made this account to follow the pattern of Pharaoh killing the babies in Egypt.[109]

Jesus then goes into exile while Herod is seeking to kill him, like Moses who goes into exile while Pharaoh is after his blood. After the death of Herod and Pharaoh, they both return (Matt 2:19–21; Exod 4:19–20). Matthew takes Hosea 11:1 "out of Egypt I have called my son," which in its original context is not messianic, and he applies it to Jesus (Matt 2:13–15). The start of the nation of Israel is now the beginning of Jesus' story.

Like the other New Testament writers, such as Paul, who reread and reinterpreted the Hebrew Bible in the light of Jesus, Matthew is convinced that Jesus recapitulates and fulfills the story of Israel. Even concerning the Mosaic law, Matthew has Jesus saying, "Do not think that I have come to abolish the law or the prophets; I have come not to abolish but to fulfill" (Matt 5:17). This positive assessment of the Mosaic law is in marked contrast to Paul, who was much more critical of the Mosaic law. It is one of many examples of Matthew's goal of describing Jesus as the fulfillment of the Hebrew Scriptures. And, as noted by many scholars, on one occasion this emphasis on fulfillment leads to weird results. In fulfillment of Zechariah 9:9, a verse that reads:

> Rejoice greatly, O daughter Zion!
> Shout aloud, O daughter Jerusalem!
> Lo, your king comes to you;
> triumphant and victorious is he,
> humble and riding on a donkey,
> on a colt, the foal of a donkey.

Matthew reads, "The disciples went and did as Jesus had directed them; they brought the donkey and the colt, and put their cloaks on them, and he sat on them" (Matt 21:6–7). Fulfillment is so precise that Matthew has Jesus riding into Jerusalem on a colt *and* a donkey.

The Gospel of Matthew is theological writing. It is telling a story (based on Mark) that has Jesus as the new Moses, the new Israel, and the promised Messiah who is the fulfillment of God's plan.

Stories of Jesus

Differing stories about Jesus go all the way back to the New Testament itself. For example, Mark's earthly Jesus differs greatly from John's. Mark has a secret Messiah who hides his divinity, whereas John has Jesus proclaiming that he is God in one of his speeches (John 8:58). At the end of Mark's Gospel, Jesus gives no simple answer to Pilate whether he is the king of the Jews (Mark 15:1–5). If this was John's Jesus, there would be no need for the trial described in Mark.

Albert Schweitzer's famous conclusion of his historical Jesus study is that after two hundred years of scholarship, almost nothing can be said about the historical Jesus, that the historical Jesus is an unknown, and that the descriptions of the historical Jesus are more pale reflections of the author than of Jesus.[110] Scholarship has progressed since Schweitzer, but the debates over who exactly was the historical Jesus and what are the right methodologies to discover this historical person are just as hotly debated today. John Dominic Crossan laments that we have "as many pictures [of Jesus] as there are exegetes, and "that stunning diversity is an academic embarrassment. It is impossible to avoid the suspicion that historical Jesus research is a very safe place to do theology and call it history, to do autobiography and call it biography."[111] What was Jesus like? What about his politics and ethics? His values and outlook? What would Jesus do? It is suspicious that most answers reflect the views of the person doing the investigation.

There are multiple stories of Jesus, and there were many more stories about Jesus that didn't make it into the New Testament. Scholars and Christian groups haven't been able to agree on Jesus. Did Jesus even historically exist? Was he a failed apocalyptic prophet? Was Jesus a feminist? Was he a political revolutionary? Was he pro-slavery? And what were his views on homosexuality? Did he rescind the Sabbath? Did he have violent tendencies or was he pacifist? Was Jesus a new Odysseus? Was Jesus a wise philosopher and moral teacher with pithy sayings? Or was he the miracle-working Son of God, the second person of the Trinity? Was Jesus a magician, a Jewish Rabbi, or a gay man? Was he a religious critic and social reformer? Perhaps Jesus was a faith healer, a prosperity guru who proclaimed a health and wealth message. Or was he the Jesus of the "fight church"—a Christian mixed martial arts church that portrays Jesus as a fighter who never gave up? Was he a man's man of many conservative churches—an outdoor, rugged, macho, patriarchal Jesus who kept women in their place? Or perhaps he was a pacifist who promoted non-violence as the appropriate response to any conflict.

Consider, for example, the debate over Jesus and women. Christian conservatives have found a Jesus to support their patriarchal views—Jesus is the *Son* of God the *Father*. Jesus appointed twelve disciples, and they were all men. Yet Christian feminists have found Jesus to be *Sophia* incarnate—the incarnation of Woman Wisdom from the Hebrew Bible and intertestamental literature. They find a Jesus who goes far beyond his culture to affirm and welcome women, and even has women be the first to testify to his resurrection. Yet still, post-Christian feminists see Jesus as one who never confronted the oppressive patriarchy of his time, and ultimately the story of Jesus is an oppressive story where a *male* savior brings salvation to all. The New Testament texts are read and interpreted differently. For instance, for some the story of Jesus with Mary and Martha (Luke 10:38–42) is evidence of Jesus affirming women. Martha complains to Jesus that her sister Mary is lazing about the house. Jesus affirms women by not telling Mary to help with "woman's housework" and allows her to continue to sit by his feet and listen to his teachings. For others, however, this story would only affirm women if a woman was teaching and a man was sitting at her feet.

Stories of Jesus move from the pacifist to the violent. If Jesus was nonviolent, didn't he overturn the tables of the money changers and do not all those who oppose the Son meet a violent and sticky end in the book of Revelation? And consider that Jesus talked about hell, punishment, and seemed to affirm violent images. He said, for example, that if your eye causes you to stumble, it is better to tear it out than have two eyes and be thrown into the eternal fire (Matt 18:8–9); that in the Parable of the Talents the worthless slave will be thrown into utter darkness where there is weeping and gnashing of teeth (Matt 25:30); that he came to bring fire to the earth and wished that it had already started (Luke 12:49); and that on the day of the Son of Man it will be like in the day Lot left Sodom and fire and sulfur rained down from heaven and destroyed everyone (Luke 17:29–30).

But perhaps when Jesus talked about hell, he was just referring to the coming destruction of Jerusalem in 70 CE? Or perhaps, because many of his teachings on hell are addressed to the religious leaders, his warnings about hell were in fact a critique against those who had consigned others to hell. The Jesus of the book of Revelation is read in opposite ways—either as one who through great battles will eventually subdue all his enemies and consign them to the lake of fire. Here Jesus is the one who leads a conquering army, with a robe dripped in blood, bringing the wrath of God (Rev 19:13–15). Or perhaps Jesus is the lamb who conquers all through sacrifice and love, whose only sword is the words that come from his mouth, and whose blood on his robes is actually *his* blood and not that of his enemies.

The myriad stories of Jesus are not all mutually exclusive, but some are. Jesus, to use Churchill's phrase about the Soviet Union, is "a riddle, wrapped in a mystery, inside an enigma." Perhaps an accurate portrayal of Jesus is the one that is contrary to what any church teaches. A lesson from Dostoyevsky's story of the Grand Inquisitor in *The Brothers Karamazov* is that when the real Jesus appears, the church rejects him. In fact, this view of Jesus is prominent in the New Testament—that whoever Jesus was, he was contrary to and subversive of the religious establishment and is finally put to death by those religious leaders.

Across the centuries, people have offered countless versions of Jesus, retold and adapted to various times and cultures. As one last example, a story of Jesus that is getting recent press is the "mythic view" of Jesus—a view that argues that stories about Jesus first began with a celestial or heavenly Jesus, and not as a historical person on earth. In this view, Paul (who authored the earliest books of the New Testament) knows little about a historical Jesus, but receives all his knowledge about Jesus through dreams, visions, and revelation. Then, much later, in the first Gospel, the writer of Mark historicizes this mythic Jesus and places him on earth.

Bart Ehrman, who argues *for* the existence of the historical Jesus, lists the evidence lacking for Jesus[112]:

1. We have no physical evidence, for example, no inscriptions or other archeological evidence.
2. We have no writings from Jesus.
3. No Greek nor Roman author from the entire first century mentions Jesus.
4. We have no contemporary eyewitness reports; no writing by anyone who was an eyewitness to what Jesus said or did.

Christians have often repeated the claim that there is more evidence for the existence of Jesus than for Julius Caesar. This idea is repeated so often that many accept it as fact, just like people once thought that heavier objects fall faster than lighter ones. For example, the New Testament scholar F. F. Bruce wrote, "The historicity of Christ is as axiomatic for an unbiased historian as the historicity of Julius Caesar."[113] You don't need to drop objects off the Leaning Tower of Pisa to show that this statement is false.

The reality is the opposite. Among the evidence for Julius Caesar, we have his likeness on coins that were minted in his lifetime. We have inscriptions, statues, and writings from several contemporary witnesses like Cicero. Significantly, we have Caesar's own writings, such as his letters and his commentaries on the Gallic Wars and the Roman Civil War. We have nothing like this for Jesus.

There are no contemporary eyewitness accounts of Jesus' life. Only towards the end of the first century are there two mentions of Jesus in Josephus—the most famous being the so-called *Testamonium Flavanium*. As an undergraduate student, I remember being impressed when told what Josephus, a Jewish historian, wrote about Jesus—that he was the Messiah who did wonderful deeds; a wise man, if indeed one could call him a man. But scholars today agree that this passage is at least in part a forgery or interpolation, and there are good arguments that Josephus wrote none of it. In any case, Josephus is not an eyewitness and finished his *Jewish Antiquities* in 93–94 CE, some sixty years after the death of Jesus, casting considerable doubt on Josephus as an independent source.

Moreover, the earliest New Testament books are written by Paul, who by his own admission was not an eyewitness of the life of Jesus but received his gospel by a revelation (Gal 1:11-12). It would be significant to have in our possession a piece of woodwork made by Jesus, draft notes to the Sermon on the Mount, a contemporary inscription memorializing a great deed of Jesus, a memoir from a family member, an account by an original disciple, a screed from a skeptic or foe, or even a brief eyewitness report from someone who actually saw and heard Jesus. But we don't. Nothing.

This lack of evidence is not a problem for Ehrman because he is not arguing for a divine miracle working Jesus, but for a Jesus who was a relatively unknown apocalyptic prophet who was crucified under the reign of Pontius Pilate. But this differs greatly from the view of Jesus portrayed in the New Testament as a famous prophet who attracted large crowds, a gadfly who raised the ire of the religious establishment, a person important enough to appear before Pontius Pilate, a miracle worker who fed five thousand people, and, most extraordinary of all, could raise the dead, and he himself was raised. One would think that someone like Philo of Alexandria, Pliny the Elder, or Seneca the Younger would have noticed and left a written record.

The mythic view says that there wasn't even a relatively unknown Jesus, never mind a well-known miracle worker.[114] Rather, it argues that the Christian movement first started with a belief in a celestial Jesus—a Jesus who communicated to his disciples by revelation, through dreams and visions, convincing them he had died and been raised in the heavenly realms. It was only later that his followers historicized the myth by placing Jesus on earth. So, for example, the authentic writings of Paul and Hebrews are read as the beginnings of the myth. Hebrews has Jesus offering himself as a sacrifice *not* on earth but in the heavenly realms (Heb 8:1-5). Hebrews doesn't quote any historical words of Jesus—there is nothing there about his teaching or deeds on earth. Also, Paul knows hardly anything of the historical Jesus and only appeals to revelations or the Scriptures (Gal 1:11-12; Rom 16:25-26). In his debates and conflicts, the reason Paul doesn't appeal to what Jesus did or said while he was alive, such as referencing Jesus' well-known parables, miracles, or sermons, is because there wasn't an original historical and earthly Jesus to base an appeal on. It is only much later that Jesus is historicized in Mark's Gospel, then copied by Matthew who adds some narratives, and then further developed by Luke and finally by John.

If the mythic view is correct, it means that all the stories about Jesus are built upon an entirely fictional creation, stories upon fictional story.

Theological stories

Christian stories are not only confined to the Bible. Theologians are storytellers, and I have some experience in this regard. My doctorate in theology through the University of South Africa, which I later revised into a book titled *The Maleness of Jesus: Is It Good News for Women?*,[115] covered several views about Jesus, and in particular the spectrum of views from patriarchal to feminist. Patriarchal theologies stress a Jesus who affirmed male leadership and authority over women. Christian feminists tell a story where Jesus undermined the patriarchal culture, and through his life and actions redefined maleness and affirmed the full equality and humanity of women. Other scholars, called post-Christian feminists, left Christianity unable to find and articulate a view of Jesus that expressed their ideas and aspirations. I for one abstracted and systematized material from the Bible, church history, science, and philosophy to tell a story that was fully inclusive of women and subversive of patriarchal narratives. But it was a story nonetheless.

Do theologians make stuff up? Yes. They retell stories, change them, and create them. This is not necessarily a death-dealing indictment. Did Chopin make stuff up? Did Shakespeare? Even in the highly precise and logical world of mathematics, there is a long-existing debate whether mathematics is invented or discovered (As a tool, my vote is that mathematics is invented). In each case, what people invent is done in communities with specific rules, conventions, and traditions.

Theological stories today differ greatly from the past. We are more likely to hear a sermon on "Sinners in the hands of a loving God" than Jonathan Edwards's "Sinners in the hands of an angry God." We could choose any doctrine of Christianity and trace its significant developments and changes across time and culture. For our example of a theological story, we will consider a central doctrine of Christianity, the atonement.

In Christian teaching, the doctrine of the atonement is central and tries to answer the questions: How can humans be at one with God? If human sin has created a great divide between God and humanity, how can we be reconciled? The presenting problem is human sin and human inability. The church, through its two-thousand-year history, has come up with various theories to explain how Jesus accomplished this atonement and reconciled people with God.

The *Christus Victor* view of the atonement is sometimes called the classic view of the atonement and held sway for the first millennium of the church's history. In this view, there is a cosmic battle between good and evil, where Christ through his death fights and conquers the ruling demonic and evil powers. Jesus' death appears to be an ultimate defeat, but his resurrection shows that the devil could not hold him. There are a couple of well-known versions of this theory: recapitulation and ransom theories.

Recapitulation is associated with Irenaeus (ca. 130–202 CE). This theory tells the story of Adam as created in the image and likeness of God, but through the devil's temptation Adam disobeyed and fell, having consequences for himself and for the entire human race. Somehow, all people were represented in Adam, so every person also fell with Adam. The answer to this problem is found in Jesus. Just as Adam represented all of humanity, and whose fall and sin corrupted all of humanity, so in Christ all of humanity is again represented, but this time Jesus lives a sinless life. In Christ, God recapitulates the story of Adam, thus now everyone is included in Christ. What we once lost in Adam, we now receive back in Christ.

The *ransom theory* is another story. Here Jesus, by his death, paid a ransom to the devil. Through the Fall in the Garden of Eden, the devil had somehow gained the rights over humanity. So God offered Jesus to Satan as a ransom for sinners. Satan agreed, but didn't realize that he couldn't hold Jesus. On the third day, Jesus rose from the dead, and the devil lost his prize. C. S. Lewis' Chronicles of Narnia exemplifies this theory, where there was a deeper magic. The white witch of Narnia thought she had finally got her grubby paws on Aslan, but beyond her knowledge was a deeper magic that brought Aslan back from the dead. Many of the church fathers had some version of this theory—Origen, Hilary of Poitiers, Augustine, and Gregory of Nyssa.

Ransom theories of the atonement made sense in "a demon-haunted world,"[116] where evil powers and the devil were thought to have remarkable power and influence. Stories such as these had currency where slavery was rampant, and "ransom" was a vital metaphor. By the Middle Ages, the culture had changed, and new theories of the atonement arose.

The *satisfaction* theory of Anselm (1033–1109) found expression in his *Cur Deus Homo* (Why did God become human?). Anselm's story is told in the context of the medieval lord of the manor and his vassals. The lord provided his vassals protection and in return vassals had obligations. When a vassal failed in his or her obligation, they offended the honor of the lord, and some satisfaction had to be given to the offended lord. Likewise, God is Lord and we are vassals. Our sin has dishonored God. Our failure, however, is not against any lord, but against God, who is infinitely greater than any other lord. Hence our infinite debt and inability to provide satisfaction to restore God's honor. No person can make this satisfaction, but because humans have dishonored God, a human must make satisfaction. Furthermore, only an infinite God can satisfy an infinite debt. Thus, through Jesus, who is both human and infinite God, can satisfaction be made. Now instead of

Jesus' death being a ransom paid to the devil, it becomes a debt that is paid to God to satisfy our obligations and restore God's honor.

In the *moral influence theory*, Abelard (1070–1142) rejected both the ransom and satisfaction theories. Abelard denied that the devil had any rights over us. Instead, he emphasized that Jesus' death was the great display of God's love, and that seeing such a wonderful display would move us to love others. The theory is about the influence or effect the death of Jesus has on a person. For Abelard, if God wants, he can just forgive. There is no need for punishment or satisfaction. This is sometimes called a subjective theory of the atonement—the atonement brings about a psychological change within us. It is about how the display of God's love awakens love in us.

By the time of Reformation, the *penal substitution theory* placed even greater emphasis on Jesus being a substitute. John Calvin modified the satisfaction theory of Anselm and developed what is one of the most well-known models of the atonement. As mentioned in chapter 2, the time of the Reformation emphasized legal frameworks and the metaphors of law, guilt, penalty, and justice had wide currency. Thus, it is unsurprising that theories of the atonement would be framed in these categories. In the penal substitution theory, sin is not so much offending the honor of the Lord (as with Anselm's theory), but a breaking of the law of God. This presents a problem. We have broken the law that requires both obedience and punishment. Because God is holy, as lawbreakers we cannot be in God's presence. And because God is just, there must be punishment for our sins. God cannot simply let the law be broken without punishment. So Jesus took the punishment that should have come to us for breaking the law. He suffered the penalty (penal) of the law and took our place (substitution).

There are many other stories of the atonement. Modern theories have thankfully moved to non-violent articulations. Feminist theologies have thoroughly critiqued violent models of the atonement as promoting an environment that supports violence, victimization, and the submission of women. The work of René Girard is another modern, non-violent example, with his theory of mimetic desires. In Girard's story, we desire what others desire; we imitate their desires, but eventually this leads to conflict because with scarce resources there are insufficient resources for everyone's desires to be met. Chaos and violence are the result. What is the solution? The community targets an individual or a group as the source of the violence—the scapegoat—and on him or her is laid all the blame for the chaos. Once this person is sacrificed, murdered, or exiled, the chaos and violence subside because people are convinced that this person was responsible—until violence rises again. According to this theory, societies seek to limit violence in three ways: through prohibitions, rituals, and scapegoating.[117] Societies try to limit violence by various rules and regulations, through rituals such as games to provide an outlet for violence (rugby, American football, boxing?), and when these can no longer contain the violence, a scapegoat—a person or group who is blamed for the society's descent into chaos—is eliminated. In this story of the atonement, God does not violently sacrifice his Son. Rather, Jesus is now the innocent scapegoat, blamed for the chaos, and eliminated to purge the violence (sins) of the society.

Many within Christianity consider the atonement to be the central doctrine of Christianity. Robert Jenson, professor of theology at Princeton Seminary, writes, "It is one of the more remarkable and remarked-upon aspects of theological history that no theory of atonement has ever been universally accepted. By now, this phenomenon is itself among the things that a proposed theory of atonement must explain."[118] It is curious that such an important doctrine of Christianity has had so many formulations and the church has never agreed on one. No worldwide council or creed has elevated one theory over another. But it makes perfect sense if we see the various atonement theories as storytelling, having the Bible as a launching point, and then using philosophical and theological ideas from the time to construct a narrative to answer the question "Why did Jesus die?" Each story focuses on select parts of the Bible, for the Bible itself doesn't emphasize just one theory. And the story keeps changing, because cultures change, because the ways people interpret the Bible change, and because the problem keeps on morphing. Is the problem the devil and his minions? Is it the offended honor of God? Is it our breaking the law of God? Is it the rising violence of a community that needs a scapegoat?

The theological stories told by Christians are vast, and even if one doesn't believe them, they are a remarkable testimony to the ingenuity, creativity, and imagination of humankind. They are dynamic stories that have changed with the writing, telling, collecting, reading, interpreting, and retelling. In short, the steps involved in developing these stories include:

- Possible eyewitnesses: Eyewitnesses are storytellers and are often notoriously unreliable.
- Oral tradition: Memories recreate the stories and alter them as they are retold.
- Authoring the books: Writing processes change, adapt, and create stories.
- Interpolations: Later editors and additions to the books further modify stories.

- Canon formation: What books included or excluded from the Bible further change and solidify the overall story.
- Biblical hermeneutics: Change how we interpret the stories.
- Bible translation: Change how we read the stories.
- Theology: Change how we tell the stories.

We should briefly mention that behind many written biblical stories is an oral tradition—an oral telling of stories that we can reasonably assume changed with the telling. In oral transmission of stories, all kinds of psychological weaknesses come into play, including our narrative creating and unreliable memories.

Then we have passages that are added later to the New Testament books. Do we include the extended version of Mark's ending as part of the story? Snake handlers in the United States find this a crucial part of the stories they tell. What about the famous story of the woman taken in adultery, another passage that was added later (John 7:53–8:11)? Is this part of the story? What about the longer version of Acts? Is 1 Corinthians 14:34–35 an interpolation, and therefore unauthentic Paul, and if so, does that change anything regarding Christian stories of women?

Then there is the history of hermeneutics, the study of how methods of interpreting the Bible have significantly changed over time, and thus changed the telling of these stories. There have been literal, allegorical, typological, tropological (moral), anagogical (mystical), grammatical-historical, theological hermeneutics, Christotelic, and other approaches to interpreting the Bible, each producing different results. When studying Romans chapter 7 at seminary, one of my New Testament professors noted that there were at least thirty different interpretations of this passage. Come to think of it, we could say this of many passages in the Bible.

Furthermore, we have the formation of the canon that took nearly four hundred years to reach some sort of consensus as people argued over what stories to include or exclude from the Bible—a debate that continued to the Reformation and beyond. From early on, there were multiple Christianities. Even Paul, in one of the earliest Christian writings, laments that some people are for Paul, some for Apollos, and some for Peter (1 Cor 1:12). There were many Epistles, Gospels, Acts, and apocalypses that didn't make it into the New Testament. For instance, there were the Gospels of Mary, Thomas, Philip, and Judas; the Acts of John, Paul, Peter, even Pilate; the epistles of Barnabus and 3 Corinthians; and the Apocalypse of Peter. Some books barely made it in, other popular works were thrown out. The Epistle of Barnabus and Apocalypse of Peter were used by many in the early churches, but in the end, they were rejected. The book of Revelation, however, was controversial for centuries and only just got in—and some churches never accepted it.

Then we have the translation of these ancient texts into modern languages. The exact meaning of these ancient texts is not transferred intact to us today. Consider the interpretive issues with the Declaration of Independence and US Constitution, relatively recent documents and written in fairly modern English. The truism "translation is treason" has currency precisely because translation changes the story in subtle and not so subtle ways. Added to this are the changes in the transmission of the text, and questions over which textual traditions do we give precedence. Do we favor the Masoretic text that only had the vowels added to the text in the tenth century, or the Dead Sea Scrolls, or the Septuagint?

Finally, we can point to the countless Christian books and articles—popular and academic—and the myriad of stories told from pulpits every Sunday. The many thousand variations of Christianity—the various denominations, churches, parachurches, home churches, and whatever else—is evidence of the diversity of these narratives and a flexibility that would impress a yoga guru.

Christianity serves as an excellent example of humankind's ability to create and multiply stories. As noted in the introduction, however, in the quest for the life worth living, the results of these Christian stories are mixed. From some stories, we have Christians promoting a message of kindness, repentance, and forgiveness. From other stories, we have Christians promoting ignorance, disharmony, and exclusion.

What should be clear is that in the quest for the good life, we need to assess carefully our stories, and (1) reject harmful stories and (2) retell and even transform fruitful stories.

Chapter 4

Transforming Stories: A Faithful Life

> The key to the future of the world is finding the
> optimistic stories and letting them be known.
>
> —Pete Seeger

> Truth is an army of metaphors.
>
> —Fredrick Nietzsche

> Faith is the most overrated virtue.
>
> —Christopher Hitchens

Don't fiddle with my favorite story!

STAR WARS GAVE PEOPLE a new myth of a long time ago in a galaxy far, far, away . . . but someone kept tampering with the story. In a 2010 film documentary titled *The People vs George Lucas*, Star Wars fans expressed both their awe and frustration with George Lucas—high praise for the creator of their wonderful myth, but riled up because Lucas kept tinkering with the story they loved.[119]

Given the popularity of Star Wars and the intensity and commitment of fans, it is not farfetched to imagine that Lucas could have turned Star Wars into a religion. In fact, Lucas's friend, the director Francis Coppola, once suggested that perhaps Lucas should do just that.[120] Chris Taylor in *How Star Wars Conquered the Universe* describes the once-a-decade census in New Zealand in 2001, where some 53,715 people listed "Jedi" as their official religion, making it the country's second largest religion. Fearing that their census would be corrupted, the Australian government threatened a $1,000 fine for all who went to the Dark Side and listed their allegiance. This didn't deter seventy thousand Australians from writing "Jedi" on their census form. But the all-time record, according to Taylor, goes to the United Kingdom, with four hundred thousand Jedi, making it the "fourth largest stated religion after Christianity, Islam, and Hinduism."[121] Lucas could have easily achieved and surpassed what L. Ron Hubbard did in creating Scientology. Hubbard, one of the most prolific science fiction writers of all time, holding a Guinness World Record for publishing 1084 books, made the achievable jump from science fiction to religion.

Even before the first Star Wars film hit theaters in 1977, Lucas was tampering with the story. According to many fans, some of the worst modifications were to come with the re-release of the original trilogy on DVD. The most egregious case was the confrontation between the bounty hunter Greedo and Han Solo in the Mos Eisley Cantina. In the original film, Han was a no-nonsense character who pulls out his gun first and shoots Greedo. Now in the special edition, Lucas has Greedo shooting first and misses. And he's a bounty hunter! And Solo is just three feet away. This changed the essence of both characters. To make matters worse, Lucas continually refused to make the original films available for sale. You can only buy the changed versions. Perhaps because of the uproar, when the Blu-ray versions were released, Lucas had tinkered again. This time Han and Greedo shoot simultaneously.

Lucas created a world, a myth, a new story that spoke to human experience, and people strongly identified with it. Whether the creator should change his or her creation is debated; but many fans revolted and continued to complain as the next three films were released with the likes of Jar Jar Binks and midichlorians—which seemed to reduce the beautiful mystical idea of the Force to a biological entity that could be scientifically measured. Given all that stories provide, it is unsurprising that we become attached to them and balk at alterations.

I love Peter Jackson's Middle Earth films, particularly his first trilogy, The Lord of the Rings. Would J. R. R. Tolkien have approved of the wizard Radagast's bunny-powered sleigh or war bats in Jackson's Hobbit trilogy? What about a female elf as a central character, and does it matter? Many think that the Hobbit movies are so bloated as to dilute the original story beyond any original flavor. Some fans of The Lord of the Rings hated the movies and thought that Jackson ruined characters, such as Faramir. They were outraged when Arwen rescued Frodo from the Nazgul. And when Sam left Frodo—that was the final straw. After all, Sam was the genuine hero of the story, and as a loyal friend, he would have never left Frodo.

J. K. Rowling has continued to add new material to the Harry Potter series on her Twitter feed and Pottermore website. Additions are sometimes fine with fans, but what about changes? Many Christians were horrified to learn that Dumbledore was gay. How could such a wise, good, and noble person be gay? Rowling, in an interview with Emma Watson, admitted she thinks Hermione Granger should have married Harry instead of Ron Weasley,[122] a change that resonates with me. In the film adaptation of the last book, *Harry Potter and the Deathly Hallows,* perhaps even the producers thought so, by having the most poignant and romantic dance in the entire series between Harry and Hermione, a vignette absent from the book.

Can the creator of the story get the story wrong? Tolkien said he didn't invent Middle Earth, he discovered it. Perhaps an author can misinterpret the nine muses. If someone has trashed your favorite story, there are "fan edit" websites and YouTube videos where you can find out the way the story should have been told.

Christianity too is littered with the aggrieved who have felt their story has been undermined. For all the arguments presented by various Christian groups for the truth of their position, an irony is sometimes lost: The central message of Jesus to the religious elite, to the keepers of the narrative, is "You got the story wrong." Jesus' words contain an inbuilt critique against the religious establishment, against those who had memorized the Scriptures but had missed life and love. It is the story that is endlessly repeated—that the religious elite get the story wrong and betray Jesus for thirty pieces of silver.

Paul also fiddled with the story. Paul spoke of his story of Jesus as being an obstacle to Jews. Many Jews did not accept Paul's message of Christianity because it departed too far from their understanding of the Hebrew Bible. Paul made radical changes. His elevation of the Abrahamic covenant above the Mosaic was a significant move. Including the gentiles into the covenant people was another. What Christians found in the Hebrew Bible was not self-evident to many.

Over the past few decades, developments in New Testament scholarship upset many evangelicals and the telling of their stories. Ever since the work of E. P. Sanders, James Dunn, and studies in Second Temple Judaism, most Pauline scholars now recognize that the Judaism of Jesus' time was not an arid legalistic religion, an ungracious system where people tried to earn their way into God's favor by their works. Although there was no monolithic Jewish view and there were many various Jewish groups, the emphasis is now that Jews endeavored to keep the Mosaic law in response to God's grace, and in fact, one could keep the law because the law also provided ways for dealing with and atoning for sin. In other words, Paul did not mean exactly what Luther, Calvin, and their descendants took Paul to mean. Paul's conversion wasn't because of a crisis of faith, where the law convicted him of sin and led him to Christ. Paul's reasoning was not from "plight to solution" but from "solution to plight"—from his experience of Christ to conclude that the Mosaic law was not ultimate nor the eventual plan of God. This "new perspective" on Paul is another notable change in the way people now read Paul.

Transforming stories

Most people perk up when they hear a delightful story. People who were lost in a talk suddenly find their way again. Those who were dozing off in class awaken. Stories grab our attention and have a captivating quality. Enjoyable books and films are good precisely because of the stories they tell.

Stories and narratives, broadly understood, are archetypes that order our thinking. They help us find meaning by connecting our life—past, present, and hoped-for future—into a narrative, with all its relationships and activities. These narratives, however, are unlike a Hollywood movie, where events tie neatly together, where everything makes sense, where the bad guys lose, where the hero or heroine has trivial flaws, or where everyone lives happily ever after. Our stories lack completeness and have many plot holes; however, our stories still help us give a rational and emotionally satisfying answer to the question: What defines my soul? Not a soul in a dualistic sense, but in the sense of what I understand to be me. Stories provide value, meaning, ethical direction, and hope to what we call the "self."

Excellent stories have a life-defining quality. We can argue that we use them to make sense of our lives and world. Cultures and societies have their own defining narratives—whether for good or ill. For instance, Hitler's National Socialism fashioned its own story to create an identity and justify its actions—a story of the Aryan race as the purest racial entity, a story that was a hodgepodge of other stories, including German nationalism, Wagner's music, Germanic mythology, Nietzsche's philosophy, and Christian antisemitism. Nations create stories that give meaning, justification, and purpose to their society. The Romans had their founding myths; the Jews have theirs. The United States has its own story; the Navajo have theirs. White apartheid South Africans had their own; Zulus have theirs. Stories constitute us and are a glue that holds our communities together.

Families and individuals also have their own defining stories, each filled with characters, plots, and conflicts, love and betrayal, tragedy and hope. These stories are foundational in that they influence how we think, how we behave, how we feel about others and ourselves.

Fruitful stories provide education and direction. They teach us something. They solve problems (Think about all the great ideas generated by science fiction). They provide hope, comfort, challenge, and inspiration. They help us with the deep questions of life—What is a good life and how do we live it? They help us figure out why it may be a good thing to apologize, or to forgive, or under what circumstances it may be virtuous to risk our lives for someone. Stories give us ways of thinking about failures and redemption, injustice and forgiveness, oppression and revolution. They can be warnings or cautionary tales—what might happen in the future (*The HandMaid's Tale, Brave New World*, or *1984*). They encapsulate what we consider valuable and what we want to pass onto the next generation.

Stories can also be transformative, with studies showing that the reading of fiction increases empathy and is one reason for the decline of violence. Naysayers about the power of literature to challenge and transform have appealed, for example, to SS soldiers at concentration camps who read Goethe—and just consider what they were like. This is unconvincing. Transformation is not automatic; neither are people entirely evil. Nazis also loved splendid music and their pets (and had progressive laws to prevent animal cruelty), but this is no argument against the transformative value of music or pets.

Stories have immense power and have the ability, like a stealth bomber, to sneak behind our defenses. Like Nathan coming to King David and telling him a story of a horrible person who stole a poor man's only sheep. Such stories can tell us things that are too hard to hear directly. Like Gulliver's travels and other satirical allegories that were too dangerous to present as direct critiques of the societies their authors inhabited.

Because we base our ways of relating and thinking on stories, with the topic of the worthwhile life, a crucial question is, "What stories are we living by?" Our lives are often a conflict of stories, one story competing with another. Like daydreamer Walter Mitty, in James Thurber's short story, we may have a fantasy world filled with stories where we are more successful, well-known, more loved, in better health, and living in peace and comfort. Life is a clash of stories, each vying for attention. In addition, the question "What stories are we living by?" is important because stories are, to use another analogy, our operating system—what loads up in the morning, and upon which everything else runs. And, like an operating system, these run in the background so that their functioning and the constraints they place on us are not always visible to us as we go about our business.

What stories do we trust to make sense of our lives? What stories give us hope and inspire us to lead a better life? What stories are excellent enough to live by? When I listened to Emma Watson's articulate and moving 2016 speech to the United Nations about women's rights,[123] I couldn't help but think she was in part channeling Hermione Granger's social activism—as seen in Hermione's quest to free the enslaved house-elves of Hogwarts.

Who can lead a life worth living? Anyone, but we need the help of good stories. Yet what might resonate with me, you may find distasteful. I am deeply moved when I watch a film or musical adaptation of Hugo's *Les Misérables*. But some people are unaffected and critical of the acting or singing. *Les Misérables* is one of the greatest stories I have read, but I am cautious of recommending books or films, because all too often a story that I find wonderful falls flat with someone else. The point is to find and tell stories that challenge and resonate with you, stories that are compelling and encourage you forward, stories that address relational failure, and give fuller meaning and motivation to love, hope, justice, and forgiveness. What is clear: we need transformative stories.

Stories are tools for living. We all live by narrative maps and use them to find our way, search for new horizons, and mark areas of importance and danger. Beyond food, water, shelter, and a smartphone, we need stories. But more than that, we need stories that are articulated in ways that promote self-awareness, humility, repentance, forgiveness, trust, love, justice, human rights, and care for the environment. Our stories need to be inclusive of all human variants, and illuminative of our effects on other beings and the larger environment we all inhabit in our incredible variety. No story does all these things well. Even our best stories have agendas. And to have continued relevance with changing times and cultures, even the best stories need transforming.

Transforming Christian stories

In our dialog with Christianity, this brings us back to the stories that Christians tell and the need for these stories to be transformed. Even Christians agree that although good has been done by those who claim to follow Jesus of Nazareth, and although horrific events in the past may have multiple causes (not just religion), there is much room for improvement. As we have seen in chapter 3, this is not asking any more than what Christians have done through their history—to change and transform their stories. In our quest for the life worth living, given that Christianity has some 2.4 billion adherents, the transformation of Christian stories is essential.

The history of Christianity is littered with sordid examples, including the persecution of Jews and promotion of antisemitism, the Crusades, witch trials, heretic burnings, persecution of heathen, religious wars, support for slavery, oppression of women, cruelty to gays, the pedophilia scandal and cover-up, support for aggressive wars, support for nationalism, support for apartheid, exploitation of people for financial gain, and corporal punishment, amongst many others. Countless times Christianity has failed to support the outsider, oppressed, or exploited. We also find climate change denial, opposition to contraception, and hostility to the findings of science. In addition, there are the many infightings between churches, denominations, and sects. There is politics and pettiness, hypocrisy and legalism. There are the endless reports of leadership abuse, and some theological formulations that sound like madness. The history of the church negates the claim that "without God any behavior is permitted." Clearly, with God any behavior is permitted. There is much room for improvement.

What do Christians say about Christianity being responsible for such widespread evils? As one representative argument, pastor Timothy Keller, in his New York Times bestseller and one of the most widely read defenses of Christianity today, *The Reason for God: Belief in an Age of Skepticism*, devotes a chapter to answering an objection to Christianity, which he titled: "The church is responsible for so much injustice." Keller notes three issues that stand out: (1) Christians' glaring character flaws, (2) Christians' support of war, injustice, and violence, and (3) the number of self-righteous and dangerous fanatics.[124]

At the outset, we should note one obvious problem—a book giving reasons to believe in God has to devote an entire chapter wrestling with why Christians are not the paragon of virtue. In fact, Keller admits that Christians often behave worse than others. It is clear even to Christians that the case for Christianity's virtue is ambiguous. Hardly a month goes by without the news announcing another church scandal. Concerning character flaws, Keller says, "Church communities seem, if anything, to be characterized by more fighting and party spirit than do other voluntary organizations . . . Church officials seem to be at least (if not more) corrupt than leaders in the world at large."[125] And on religious violence, he says, "Violence done in the name of Christianity is a terrible reality and must be both addressed and redressed. There is no excusing it. In the twentieth century, however, violence has been inspired as much by secularism as by moral absolutism."[126] Unfortunately, that last sentence sounds like an excuse and is a misuse of the term "secularism." Secularism, by insisting on keeping the state and religion separate, has not incited violence but rather protected all citizens under the law and provided a foundation for modern democratic societies.

Keller provides common and representative answers that Christians give to the problematic behavior of many Christians throughout history:

1. There are nominal Christians, people who are not Christian enough, and self-righteous extremists.[127] The Bible, however, critiques this self-righteous religion and Jesus himself opposes these types of people.

2. Keller speaks of "common grace." (This is a concept in some Christian theologies that claims that God empowers every good deed.) Thus, if we find a contrast in behavior, where non-believers are better than those in the church, God's grace is also behind these virtuous deeds of non-Christians.

3. Christian teaching speaks of the "seriously flawed character of real Christians."[128] Yes, there are imperfect Christians, but they might be a lot worse if they weren't Christian. In addition, it is those with flawed characters that see their need for God, so "we should expect that many Christians' lives would not compare well to those of the nonreligious."[129]

4. Non-Christians have done terrible things as well, including atrocities by Russian, Chinese, and Cambodian communist regimes of the twentieth century.

5. There have been Christians who have done good. Keller mentions William Wilberforce, Dietrich Bonhoeffer, Martin Luther King Jr., and Desmond Tutu.[130]

Taking these points out of order, point 3 is simply further confirmation of the problem. To admit that Christians are seriously flawed misses the salient point—that Christianity claims to be radically transformative—and raises the question of what use Christianity is in this world. To say that people could be worse if they weren't Christians is a weak argument. It's just as probable that they would be better. The argument dips into the realm of the counter-factual "what if?" Would this person be worse if they weren't a Christian? Perhaps they would be much better. Many people who left Christianity consider themselves to have become better people. Many abandoned Christianity because of where the quest for truth and love led them, and because they tired of Christianity's exclusivity. The counter-factual argument can go both ways, but the fact remains that we have the admitted, seriously flawed characters of many Christians, never mind that they could be worse.

Similar with point 4. No one disputes that non-Christians have done horrendous things. Although we can debate whether these evil actions were motivated by a non-belief in supernatural entities (highly unlikely), by ideologies, personality cults, nationalism, or by something else. This point again side-steps the problem that we have already mentioned: the message of Christianity claims to be profoundly transformative and to promote the life worth living. Why don't Christians behave better? It is no defense to one's own wrongdoing to distract and appeal to how terrible someone else is. In the Nuremberg trials, Hermann Goering once piped up about the United States massacre of American Indians. Perhaps Goering got the idea from Hitler, who himself had learned much from the United States' treatment of Native Americans. Goering's comment fell flat. One of the legal points made before the Nuremberg trials got underway was that those being tried for war crimes were not allowed to argue, "Well, the Allies did terrible things as well." It's no defense.

Point 5 is agreed upon by most as well. Although, perhaps these people are or were simply good people and would have done great good even if they weren't Christian. But we grant their Christianity propelled them to do good. Christianity has surely motivated people toward love and justice. The problem is that we can easily find other people who have used the Bible for hatred and breeding social discord. In other words, kind people use the Bible in good ways, and nasty people in evil ways. Some find in the Bible reasons for compassion, equality, and love, while others find reasons to exclude, subordinate, and divide.

Furthermore, the people that Keller mentions—Wilberforce, Bonhoeffer, King, and Tutu—are held up as examples of how good Christianity is, but sadly they are rather lonely islands in a sea of considerable opposition from large numbers of Christians and churches. In other words, Keller mentions Christians who were exceptions, which makes the problem more acute. With each remarkable person, we should remind ourselves of how many other Christians have acted.

Tutu encountered massive resistance from many churches and Christians in apartheid South Africa—one that called itself a Christian county. The English denomination that I belonged to in South Africa during apartheid prided itself in supporting the status quo and used to display banners across the highway declaring "We don't preach politics." The large Afrikaans denominations even made a biblical case for apartheid—using passages such as Acts 17:26, "From one ancestor he made all nations to inhabit the whole earth, and he allotted the times of their existence and the boundaries of the places where they would live." Apartheid was justified because God had created the distinct races and had designated a different or separate region to each one. Like sexist theologies that use the curse on Eve to be ruled by her husband to justify patriarchy (Gen 3:16), apartheid theology used the curse on Canaan, to be the lowest of slaves, to justify the subordination of black people (Gen 9:25–27).

Bonhoeffer also is an exception and reminds us that Christianity is complicit with Nazi Germany. We only have to read Martin Luther's tome *On the Jews and Their Lies* to find an example of Christianity's vile promotion of antisemitism. Luther dehumanized Jews by calling them liars, thieves, fools, lazy, blind, stupid, and the devil's children. He called for setting fire to their synagogues, houses, and books. He urged confiscating their money and property, showing them no mercy, forbidding them to teach, and consigning them to slave labor or exile. The Nazis obliged, and more.

When the Nazi party came to power, 97 percent of Germans considered themselves to be Christians.[131] (A shocking and sobering statistic, like Rwanda, which before the 1994 genocide had a population of 90 percent Christian.) Were most churches and Christians opposed to Hitler coming to power in 1933? No, they enthusiastically voted for him and gave moral permission to the nation to support the Nazi regime. Historian Robert Ericksen extensively documents this in *Complicity in the Holocaust: Churches and Universities in Nazi Germany*. As an example, he writes: "Paul Althaus, a professor of theology at the University of Erlangen and probably the leading Luther expert of his day, proclaimed in 1933, 'Our Protestant churches have greeted the turning point of 1933 as a gift and miracle of God.'"[132]

Many Christians viewed Hitler as one who stood for their values and one who would return Germany to greatness and traditional lifestyles. But that was 1933 (although it was clear even then that the Nazi party was brutal). What about later? Most Christians supported Hitler's tearing up of the Versailles Treaty, the remilitarization of the Rhineland, the annexation of Austria, the invasion of Czechoslovakia, and in 1939 when Hitler waged aggressive war and his blitzkrieg shattered Poland, "Catholic and Protestant churches designated an entire week in which church bells should be rung in celebration."[133] Ericksen concludes, "Most historians today acknowledge the heroism of Niemöller and Bonhoeffer, but they also argue that it misrepresents the story of the churches. These two men represented a small and radical wing of a large church that found much to like in the Nazi state."[134]

Wilberforce and the movement to end slavery reminds us of the multitudes in the Christian pro-slavery movement, particularly in the American south. Pro-slavery apologists found considerable justification for slavery from the Hebrew Bible and the New Testament.

The great abolitionist Frederick Douglass recounts a time in his early life in bondage, when his owner converted to Christianity:

> I indulged a faint hope that his conversion would lead him to emancipate his slaves, and that, if he did not do this, it would, at any rate, make him more kind and humane. I was disappointed in both these respects. It neither made him to be humane to his slaves, nor to emancipate them. If it had any effect on his character, it made him more cruel and hateful in all his ways; for I believe him to have been a much worse man after his conversion than before. Prior to his conversion, he relied upon his own depravity to shield and sustain him in his savage barbarity; but after his conversion, he found religious sanction and support for his slaveholding cruelty.[135]

Douglass described how his master became influential in the church, converted others, prayed morning, noon, night, and continued to whip slaves until bleeding—all while quoting Scripture. His damning conclusion regarding Christian slaveholders is this: "For of all slaveholders with whom I have ever met, religious slaveholders are the worst. I have ever found them the meanest and basest, the most cruel and cowardly, of all others."[136]

Finally, regarding Martin Luther King Jr., we can refer to his well-known *Letter from a Birmingham Jail*, which was a critique of other Christian ministers for their support of the racist status quo. King's letter, which opened with "My Dear Fellow Clergymen," was a response to eight white local clergymen who had accused King of being an extremist and an outsider. Did most white clergy and churches in the American South rise in support and solidarity with Martin Luther King Jr.? No. This lack of support was one of King's greatest disappointments. In a 1965 interview, a few years before his death in 1968, King was asked to reflect on any mistakes he had made in the civil rights movement. King replied, "Well, the most pervasive mistake I have made was in believing that because our cause was just, we could be sure that the white ministers of the South, once their Christian consciences were challenged, would rise to our aid. I felt that white ministers would take our cause to the white power structure. I ended up, of course, chastened and disillusioned."[137] Exceptional Christians are often just that—exceptions.

Returning to Keller's five points, point 2 is an all too convenient argument. It attempts to soften the blow that we find good people outside of Christianity and nasty people within Christianity. What is Keller's answer? The good that we see outside of Christianity is because of Christianity (God's grace), but the bad within Christianity is because humans are flawed. But if God is helping those outside Christianity to be good, why doesn't God help Christians to be much better? In this argument, the good outside Christianity doesn't show us up, it simply shows that God is at work outside our religion. We take credit for good everywhere. In addition, this argument clashes with other teachings in the New Testament that unbelievers are dead in their sins, deluded, corrupt, without hope, live in darkness, get up to all kinds of mischief and sin, and need salvation.

This leaves point 1, which is usually the most common answer from Christians—that those committing atrocities and doing evil are not real or genuine Christians. What about this crooked pastor, the abuse in the Catholic church, the Crusades, Inquisition, religious wars, slavery, oppression of women, the history of antisemitism, or homophobia? Well, they weren't real Christians, or at least if they were Christians, they weren't following the example of Jesus. Jesus himself opposed this type of behavior. This answer is better, but still fallacious. Richard Dawkins once wrote an article titled "Atheists for Jesus,"[138] where he expressed an admiration for the ethics of Jesus. Although one should be selective about what teachings of Jesus to admire, I grant that there is a generally accepted view that Jesus forgave, and spoke about mercy, the golden rule, and love, and that he welcomed the outsider and confronted the religious leaders of his day. But the argument of point 1 is fallacious because the problem is so *widespread*. The argument could work if character flaws and violence were limited. It would make sense if these nominal Christians were isolated cases, but broad swaths of Christianity are implicated.

Take, for example, the question of human rights. When it comes to slaves, antisemitism, women, blacks, LGBTQ, and rights for children, most don't immediately think of a mass of churches at the forefront of affirming and fighting for these rights. In fact, much of Christianity still denies women leadership positions; many conservative Christians still use corporal punishment on their children; much of the opposition to gays comes from the religious; Luther's antisemitism is just one example of many of Christian persecution and pogroms against the Jews; and even Christian abolitionists in the nineteenth century needed to adopt new hermeneutical methods to argue that gospel themes such as love, freedom, and image of God, were more important than the specific biblical texts that authorized the institution of slavery.

People worldwide have often asked with surprise, "How could so many Christians support Donald Trump?" And given the omnishambles that accompanied Trump's tenure as president, how could Christians continue to support him? Trump, who by any rational account, is immoral, incompetent, immature, and ignorant of too many things, received 81 percent of the white evangelical vote in 2016, and it is safe to say, he wouldn't have been elected without their vote. But given what we have seen of Christian support for patriarchy, slavery, the Nazi party, homophobia, and other examples, the evangelical Faustian bargain with Trump was unsurprising. For each of the above cases these Christians have claimed the moral high ground, but if they just looked down, they would see, like Wiley E Cayote, that they are already over the cliff. Power, identity, patriarchy, nationalism, promises of protection, and one's pocketbook are powerful motivators.

"They aren't real Christians" is a no-true-Scotsman fallacy—a fallacy attributed to the philosopher Antony Flew. In his book *Thinking Straight*, Flew imagined a Scotsman, who upon reading in his Sunday newspaper a report about a terrible deed committed by a sex-manic Englishman, exclaimed, "No Scot would do such a thing." Next Sunday, however, the Scotsman reads of an actual Scotsman who did something more horrible, and he retorts, "No *true* Scotsman would do such a thing."[139] Who gets to define a true Scotsman? It's like asking "Who is a real American?" No one has a claim to say who are the real Christians. Although each group claims, we are true Christians; we have the full gospel; we have the Catholic tradition; we have the Reformed truth that sets us apart; we have the charismatic gifts of the Spirit; we represent the genuine spirit of Jesus. Christianity has always been Christianities, even from its birth, with multiple stories in its foundational texts. There have always been multiple understandings of Christianity. Who is the *true* Christian? No one knows.

Christian stories need transforming for at least three significant reasons:

1. Given that Christianity has some 2.4 billion adherents, the transformation of Christian stories is essential. The stories told throughout the history of Christianity have often led to relational failure and therefore have undermined the quest for the life worth living. We need not repeat the list of these evils. Some doubt whether it is possible to transform these stories, for when they look at the Bible, they see, "one long celebration of violence."[140] Are the foundational stories in the Bible so terribly enculturated with its wars, violence, immorality, genocide, polygamy, slaves, patriarchy, and creationism, to provide any value today? But then again, many Christians have found an inbuilt critique in the Bible and remarkable surprises for that ancient culture, for example, in the Song of Songs, the figure of Woman Wisdom in Proverbs, 1 Corinthians 13, the Parables of the Prodigal Son and Good Samaritan, and views of God that over time have changed from extremely violent to more merciful.

2. Times and cultures change. Therefore, stories need to change to make sense and to be relevant in the new time and place. This should be uncontroversial because, as already seen in chapter 3, Christians have continually changed the stories they tell and haven't been content with just repeating the formulations of the past. These stories were more compelling in the past, where many gods were vying for attention, in a "demon-haunted

world" where supernatural entities played havoc on the seas and with crops, where diseases and disorders were caused by demons, where sacrifices were commonplace, where witches had supernatural powers to commit much wickedness, and where there was a lack of scientific answers. Given our understanding in the twenty-first century, Christians have even more reason to rework their stories.

3. Christians themselves are troubled by aspects of their stories. John Calvin, who is known for his teachings on predestination,[141] called the predestination of the wicked to eternal torment a horrible decree.[142] C. S. Lewis wrote that if there was one doctrine that he could get rid of, it would be the doctrine of hell.[143] Pro-slavery apologists grudgingly admitted that slavery was ultimately contrary to the gospel and the purposes of God.[144] Some who hold to patriarchal positions have admitted they would like to adopt an egalitarian position, but their views on the Bible don't allow it.[145] Homophobic Christians routinely emphasize that they love gays and have gay friends. Clearly, Christians are ethically conflicted by many of their stories. In addition, there are Christians who, in light of modern science and culture, have already significantly transformed stories of the past, including the creation stories, patriarchal narratives, violent narratives, stories on the virgin birth and ascension into heaven of Jesus, and doctrines on the soul, penal substitutionary atonement, and hell.

Of course, some Christian groups try to petrify the story as it was told in ages gone by, and who in the modern world construct quaint medieval forts with archers on the battlements to defend against the barbarians. This, however, is no longer a transformative story that meshes and connects with the twenty-first century, but a vestigial theology, a remnant of something that was once perhaps useful. In these forts we find people defending the Bible at every point, leaving people trapped in an offensive world that no longer makes sense and is no longer good news.

All Christians, however, have adapted their stories, going back to the apostle Paul, whom scholars have increasingly realized is a storyteller. In the authentic letters of Paul, the earliest writings of the New Testament, we have Paul reconfiguring and rereading the Hebrew Bible in the light of Jesus. We only have to read Paul in Galatians chapters 3 and 4 to see that Paul isn't doing a grammatical-historical interpretation of the Hebrew Bible. There he reads the ancient stories of Hagar and Sarah as allegories, where Hagar represents Mount Sinai and slavery, and Sarah refers to the freedom of the heavenly Jerusalem. Paul reinterprets Hebrew Bible passages in the light of what he believes to be a larger context—the end or goal of the story to which each passage belongs, the story of Christ.

In Paul, there is a clear distinction between the authorized text and the story he was telling. This essential distinction between text and story wasn't unique to Paul. The early church argued for the inclusion of the gentiles, even when their text—the Hebrew Bible—excluded gentiles. The early Christians (Acts 15) solved the gentile "problem" not by appealing to the so-called "clear texts" of their Scripture but by arguing that God through Jesus and the Spirit's work was now doing something new. It was not harkening back to the way things were, but rather arguing that there was a new development in Jesus. This approach eventually led to the relativization and redefinition of the Torah. A similar methodology enabled Christian abolitionists in the nineteenth century to argue that although the text of Scripture did not condemn the institution of slavery, the gospel story did—with its message of freedom, love, and the equality of all people.

The transformation of Christianity can be achieved even by using the material in its own stories. Jesus transformed the story. Paul transformed the story. And Christians continue to do so. From game theory, we saw that human cooperation and achieving outcomes where all parties benefit depends on trust, repentance, forgiveness, clarity of intentions, and repercussions against relational failure. Christian stories can include these and more. In other words, there are Christian stories that contain the essentials for transformation—disruption, self-examination, repentance, forgiveness, love, seeking the truth, justice, sacrifice, including the outsider, and relational faithfulness.

Christianity would trouble few people if it were remarkably transformative, if it lived up to its best ideals. Today, however, there are still too many times people ask, "Why don't Christians behave better?" There are still too many Christians opposing science, making unreasonable and implausible assertions about the world, and not being open to the possibility of being wrong. The Judeo-Christian tradition harkens back to the call of Abraham to be a light to the gentiles. But what happens when the gentiles possess the light? Can Christian stories embrace that, or are they always right and does everyone else live in darkness?

We all need stories that encourage skepticism and the possibility that we are the easiest people to fool, that we get things wrong, make mistakes, and often need a healthy dose of disruption to aid the process of change.

Christian stories are obviously important for Christians, but I will argue that these stories are important and valuable even if one doesn't believe they are true in the sense of having a supernatural agent behind these stories. We can all have an interest in these stories and their transformation. We can find some shared goals and desires.

In a well-known two-hour discussion[146] between the atheists Daniel Dennett, Christopher Hitchens, Richard Dawkins, and Sam Harris, toward the end the conversation, they talked about Christian stories. Dennett spoke about his annual Christmas party and the singing of carols—not the secular ones, but the Christian, and remarked that it is glorious stuff and a fantastic story. Dawkins spoke on one of his favorite pieces of music: Bach's *Mache dich, mein Herze, rein*, and emphasized that it was not just the music that is so moving, but the words and what it means. The music and art inspired by these Christian stories has many adherents outside Christianity. David Randolph, who conducted Handel's *Messiah* at Carnegie Hall every year from 1965 to a year before his death in 2010, and who performed the Messiah a remarkable 173 times in his career, was an atheist.

Many outside Christianity love these stories and music as they would love a splendid piece of fiction. Biblical books are still found in courses on great literature in secular universities. Norway is often held up as an example of a secular society that has created one of the most just, caring, and fruitful societies. What was Norway's bestselling book in 2011? A new translation of the Bible that even outsold *Fifty Shades of Grey*.[147] At least we can agree that they are remarkable stories, with enough substance and diversity to keep people interested; a testimony to the creative religious imagination of humanity that two thousand years have passed and some 2.4 billion people still claim an allegiance to these stories, and many others find deep enjoyment in them.

Clearly, non-Christians can also find rich meaning and value in Christian stories. Part of those riches is the substance that these stories give to our metaphors and analogies—which form the basis for our thinking and speaking. From a young child to the greatest scientist, all think and reason by metaphor and analogy. We couched everything we say or write in metaphor, and to refute this idea, you would have to use metaphors.

The world would be far poorer without the metaphorical power of words such as "trust," "humility," "forgiveness," "repentance," "heaven," "angels," "Eden," "incarnation," "resurrection," "atonement," "sacrifice." These central themes of Christianity are not uniquely Christian, but have been given depth and content through its stories and fueled the imaginations of musicians, artists, and authors. Even atheist writers use these metaphors in some of their book titles, for example, *River Out of Eden* and *A Devil's Chaplain* by Richard Dawkins, *The Better Angels of Our Nature* by Steven Pinker, and *Knocking on Heaven's Door* by Lisa Randall.

Religious imagination is part of our humanity and, as far as we can tell, was with us from the appearance of Cro-Magnon. Religious stories can give meaning and substance to concepts vital to the good life. Thus, these stories, if continually transformed, can aid us in the quest for the life worth living.

Where will Christian stories end up if they undergo the radical transformation necessary for telling in the twenty-first century so that they aid justice, truth, love, and contribute to ethical discussions? Christian stories do have ingredients available for transformation—disruption, self-examination, repentance, accepting the truth, and including the outsider. But whatever stories are told, in order to promote the life worth living, they need to stand up to tests and questioning, and where they claim to be true, they need to mesh with reality as we know it. And given that our understanding of "reality" evolves, these stories will need constant revision.

Given its history, Christianity needs ways to reject its destructive stories—with greater speed, intention, self-awareness, and energy. And it needs ways to continue to transform its beneficial stories. To promote the life worth living, Christianity needs ways of evaluating stories and rejecting the rotten. To accomplish this, and in keeping with our emphasis on relational thinking, I'd suggest a relational test.

A relational test

Different fields of inquiry have different criteria for separating the wheat from the chaff. Scientists have their scientific methods, control groups, and double-blind experiments to help remove human bias. We can attribute part of the success of science to its methods that can weed out delusion, cognitive biases, fallacious reasoning, and incorrect subjective impressions. Built into scientific procedures is the recognition that we are all have our biases and delusions, and we need checks and balances. The motto of the Royal Society is *nullius in verba*—"take no one's word for it." Theories can be affirmed, changed, or falsified based on evidence, observation, repeated experimental confirmation, and peer review.

Historians have a separate set of criteria for determining whether a past event happened. They cannot repeat the event or duplicate the results, but historians have many criteria to justify a claim that an event in the past most probably happened. For example, does the event under question naturally happen in the world? And is there evidence such as coins, inscriptions, papyruses, eyewitness accounts, statues, or multiple independent sources? For instance, historians can supply good reasons, based on documents, artifacts, and known events, why they think Julius Caesar almost certainly existed and crossed the Rubicon River in 49 BCE.

Music also has different criteria for determining a wonderful piece of music. These are different criteria from scientists and historians, but musicians provide reasons, for example, why Bach's forty-eight preludes and fugues and Beethoven's thirty-two sonatas are held in such high esteem and considered the Old and New Testaments of piano music. Likewise, experts in literature can tell us why they think the works of Shakespeare, Austen, Flaubert, Dickens, or Tolstoy are great literature. And art experts can explain why the works of Kandinsky, Monet, Van Gogh, Rembrandt, Caravaggio, or Michelangelo are counted among the world's greatest. We may say that there is an inter-subjective agreement among experts and others what makes up splendid music, art, or literature.

Of course, none of these determinations are infallible and may change. Everything is provisional and open to revision. There is no foundation of certainty. The Impressionists were once ridiculed, but today are counted among the greatest artists. Today, we recognize the extreme difficulty in deciding what is outstanding music, art, or literature. Even in the sciences, there are many examples where the ostensible data- and evidence-driven disciplines have failed miserably. But that has not stopped us from trying, which leads us to consider tests for religious stories.

What about religious stories, and in particular, the stories Christians tell? Are some like an awful piece of music or a horrific tale, like eugenics, lobotomies, or the recovered memory movement? Some are, and Christianity needs ways to jettison outdated, harmful, obnoxious views and beliefs. In the quest for the life worth living, we need stories that continually challenge themselves to be self-correcting.

It shouldn't be "This is my story, and that's reality," or "You have to accept this by faith," or "The Spirit testifies that this is correct," or "This logically fits into my system" (Almost anything you can imagine can be made logically possible). If the story is so important and life-changing, there need to be better tests upon which we can have some measure of agreement. Tests cannot resort to an unassailable failsafe "faith," "personal experience," "Spirit testimony," or "visions or dreams."

There are countless stories that Christians tell, and we have noted many in the previous chapters. Some stories are certainly toxic, even deadly. There were those end-time prophecies where the world will end in 1982, then 1998, then 2001, etc. Some people attached to these stories, in anticipation, sold all their possessions and ruined their lives. Some tell stories that include destructive death wishes upon everyone except their tribe. There are Christian snake handlers who fixate on the story at the end of Mark, who handle poisonous snakes and suffer needless deaths. There are parents who refuse medical attention for their children because their Christian story tells them to only trust God and pray. There are gay-haters like the American pastor Scott Lively who was once charged in federal court for crimes against humanity, for his role in the "kill the gays" movement in Uganda. Where did he get his story? There are churches that, through their storytelling, rake in vast quantities of money and endow their pastors with obscene wealth and million-dollar smiles. We have some seminaries and Christian universities that appear not to have taken a breath of fresh air for decades and have so isolated themselves that their echo chamber has convinced them they can speak with authority on every academic field. These institutions supply many examples of the Dunning-Kruger effect—a cognitive bias where one overestimates one's competence. The stories told in these institutions present minor challenge or disruption to this cognitive bias or to the collective mindset where arrogance is a virtue, shallow thinking is unchallenged, and hostility to outsiders is prized. Faculty who question the story or push the boundaries are booted out and deprived of livelihood.

Now there are wonderful stories, but as noted previously, this is no excuse for the bad. We have already mentioned Desmond Tutu and how his Christianity inspired and directed his reconciliatory work. There are countless untold and unknown stories, such as the Christian woman who with no recognition devotes her time to aiding the elderly. We have Christians who have started hospitals, orphanages, educational institutions, and organizations to promote justice and wellbeing around the world. There are many churches that help the sick, poor, and homeless. There are also liberation theologies that have emphasized God's preferential option for the poor; feminist and womanist theologies that tell stories that address the marginalization and abuse of women; and abolitionist stories that exposed the evils of slavery.

Of course, many Christians are horrified by the extremists among them, are perhaps mildly amused by the more benign Christian groups, and take credit for the good examples. The problem is not in the number of stories, but in the type or content of those stories. For Christianity to promote the life worth living, it would be helpful to have a more upfront, self-conscious, agreed-upon test to weed out the bad and to clarify what stories are rubbish and harmful. For Christianity to claim to be transformative and to promote the good life, it needs to show that it is meeting these claims. Although it may be too much to hope, each Christian group should have tests, checks and balances, ways of deciding what among its myriad of stories to keep and what to consign to the garbage.

Let's consider a *relational test*—a test that is derived from central teachings in Christian stories, indeed even required by them. We could choose an ethical theory or combination of theories as a test, such as consequentialism (best consequences and wellbeing for all) or utilitarianism (whatever maximizes happiness and minimizes suffering) or virtue ethics (a focus on a person's character) or deontological ethics (duty to the law). Although many Christians would find places of agreement with the above theories, this would cause a problem for many Christians who resist theories, criteria, or values imposed from the outside. In addition, it would be good to see whether Christianity has resources within its own stories for its transformation. So let's use Christianity's own claims as the test, not limiting ourselves to specific biblical texts themselves, because, as is well-known, people have picked and selectively chosen texts from the Bible to justify all manner of sins, including murder.[148]

A relational test starts by asking whether Christian stories are compatible with generally acknowledged central themes of Christianity. By most accounts, when Christians are asked about the core and essential teachings of Jesus, or of the New Testament, examples are given such as love, forgiveness, truth, freedom, justice, including the outsider, and helping people regardless of rules or religious authorities. Stories such as the most well-known parables, The Prodigal Son, the Good Samaritan, and the Unmerciful Servant are mentioned, and each reinforce the themes of mercy, love, forgiveness, and the goodness of outsiders. Jesus, as one sent from God, is known for socializing with sinners, tax collectors, and diseased outcasts. Whatever people make of the stories of Jesus' death, there is a general agreement that he did it for others, that his death came about because of his concern for the underdog and standing up to the religious authorities. People also mention exemplary passages from Paul. For two examples: Paul's description of love in 1 Corinthians 13:4–6: "Love is patient; love is kind; love is not envious or boastful or arrogant or rude. It does not insist on its own way; it is not irritable or resentful; it does not rejoice in wrongdoing, but rejoices in the truth"; and Paul's list of worthy things in Philippians 4:8: "Whatever is true, whatever is honorable, whatever is just, whatever is pure, whatever is pleasing, whatever is commendable, if there is any excellence and if there is anything worthy of praise, think about these things." In fact, for Paul, love sums up the entire law (Gal 5:14) and he urges to "test everything; hold fast to what is good" (1 Thess 5:21).

In addition, within the biblical stories themselves, we find a relational test. Jesus said emphatically, "By their fruits you will know them" (Matt 7:16), and asks those who claim to follow him, "Why do you call me 'Lord, Lord,' and do not do what I tell you?" (Luke 6:46). The relational test specifically relates to how you treat those outside your group, "for if you love those who love you, what reward do you have?" (Matt 5:46). The test is not "claims of faith" or mere words, but love. In 1 John 3:18 we read, "Let us love, not in word or speech, but in truth and action." Likewise, the letter of James emphasizes that claims of faith are useless without accompanying good works and love. One cannot claim to believe and not have the virtuous deeds to back up that claim of faith. There is a relational test and the evidence to pass this test is love.

The emphasis on "love," however, can sound quite general and nebulous, and Christians have been known to redefine "love" to mean just about anything.[149] Can we narrow down some specific cases? In two thousand years, the church has weeded out some stories that have choked the life out of people. In other words, Christian groups have already used the relational test and rejected toxic stories that failed relationally. I'm not suggesting anything new. In nineteenth-century North America, Christians fought for decades between abolitionist and pro-slavery views. Each used the Bible to establish their position—for or against the institution of slavery. The debate wasn't decided by an appeal to the Bible, but through a Civil War and a change in culture that eventually came to view slavery as morally reprehensible. On another level, however, Christian abolitionists swamped the opposition. Most Christians now agree that the gospel themes highlighted by abolitionists—freedom, love, equality—are more important than some biblical texts that justify the institution of slavery. Christians also now agree that some biblical stories are more important than others, for instance, that the Exodus from Egypt is a better metaphor for liberation than the conquest of Canaan![150] But more than that—the pro-slavery position failed the relational test by undermining the wellbeing and harmony between people, by denying love, by trampling human rights, and by establishing inequalities in relationships and thus promoting violence and social discord.

Similarly, Christians now agree that apartheid South Africa, which was propped up by biblical stories, failed the relational test. Christians on both sides had their favorite texts. Was it Romans 13—where everyone should obey the government because they are God's servants? Or was it Revelation 13—where the government is a vicious beast and following it is to fall into idolatry? The debate wasn't solved over biblical interpretation. Over time, Christians have ruled out theological stories that have resulted in relational failure. This is an essential point that deserves repeating: in the end, Christians have not rejected stories because of a particular interpretation of the Bible or a decree from a pope, but on whether these stories are relationally fruitful or destructive. (And these rejections occurred not in isolation, but in a particular time and culture—a culture that may well have spurred the church to change.) Appeals to the Bible didn't work, as it should be obvious today because through two thousand years people have been able to derive all sorts of mischief from the Bible. *Sola Scriptura* (Scripture alone) is a failed attempt as an authoritative test.

The same conclusion should be reached regarding the gender debate. Christians spent decades arguing over whether women and men are equal, having the same rights (such as rights to leadership), and whether women should be submissive in the family. Once again, no consensus was reached regarding the biblical texts. Various positions used the Bible to justify their arguments. There was no winner on an interpretative level and many churches still deny women leadership positions. The relational test, however, affirms that feminist interpretations and stories are good, just, and the way forward. Similar to pro-slavery and apartheid, patriarchy fails the relational test by denying women full human rights, squandering their abilities and contributions, denying them control over their bodies, promoting inequality in relationships that often leads to violence and poverty, assigning them to a subordinate status, and generally making women miserable.

The fights over slavery, apartheid, or women are resolved through a relational test. The test is not over who can prove their position from the Bible. What is conclusive is the relational evidence and results.

The relational test therefore says that any theological story that ends up endorsing sin (relational failure) is contrary to the central claims of Christianity itself—that any view endorsing slavery, apartheid, genocide, aggressive wars, killing "witches," persecuting heretics, oppressing women, inciting violence toward gays, or denying human rights—has failed the relational test. Sadly, we have to even include genocide, for Christian apologists like William Craig see the stories of the Canaanite genocides as morally justifiable, and "pity" the people who were commanded by God to slaughter everyone, including women and children.[151]

Other aspects of the relational test would include being in good and symbiotic relationship with the environment. Some Christian stories fail this test by denying that humans can do anything disastrous to the world because God oversees and controls everything. Theological stories that continue to neglect or ignore our considerable deleterious effect on the environment are incapable of dealing with this example of sin—relational failure with our environment.

In addition, part of the relational test is being in good relationship to the truth, as we know it today. This relationship will change as our understanding of what is true changes. Again, the central teachings of the New Testament stress the importance of the truth: speaking the truth, seeking the truth, knowing the truth, and following Jesus who is called the Truth. The relational test includes the test of whether the stories are in accordance with what we know about the world today. We are not talking about conformity to esoteric and debated theories such as string theory or multiple universes, but generally-agreed-upon reality. Stories or parts of stories that claim to be non-fiction need to be grounded in what we know today. Otherwise, we are becoming delusional, having lost contact with reality. (Of course, we may keep fictional stories, and they can be useful for a good life, but we must recognize and acknowledge that they are fictional.) This is nothing less than to say that the quest for the life worth living must accept the truth, that truth cannot be a casualty in the process of transformation, and that disruption be given the opportunity to open our eyes to the possibility that we might be wrong. We all must be open to the skeptical question—to interrogation and analysis whether what we are saying is true. The relational test includes a reality test: are we in relationship with the truth as we are reasonably sure of it today?

A life worth living is surely a life that seeks what is true. But truth is often subtle, elusive, and easily missed. Truth is sometimes hard to face. Finding truth takes coaxing and demanding work, the opposite of apologetic arguments that are simply speaking to the converted and defending something to which one is already committed. Too many Christians operate on the assumption that they already possess the truth, so they can pontificate to historians, philosophers, geneticists, paleontologists, evolutionary biologists, sociologists, or whoever else. Too many Christians oppose academic fields where they have no competence, qualification, or recognized authority. Such feeble positions fail the relational test regarding truth and honesty, and stymie opportunities for transformation.

Although this book focuses on Christianity, we can apply a relational test to other groups. Lawrence Wright's devastating exposé of Scientology clearly shows that most of this cult fails a relational test, with its abuse, violence, internal prisons, and money grabbing totalitarian leaders.[152] If a religious story encourages people to fly planes into buildings, behead people, or kill cartoonists, it should be universally condemned. This test also applies to the non-religious as well and their stories. Several prominent atheists have been accused of harassment, assault, abuse, and misogyny.[153] Clearly, relational failure isn't limited to Christian believers.

We need a relational test because we can get our stories wrong. Stories involve our faults, desires, and weaknesses, and therefore need to be relationally tested: Is what I'm saying kind? And is what I'm saying true? We all have our delusions. From our heritage, we all can fall into racism, classism, and sexism. Part of the success of modern science is because of an insistence on rigorous checks and balances, as well as precise and testable predictions. Yes, there are cases of fraud and scientists cheating their results, but science is self-regulating and has built-in tests to help uncover such cases.

Religions need a religious method—a relational test—that can double and triple check the evidence to ensure that fanatics, charlatans, narcissists, and psychopaths don't end up manipulating thousands of people for their own power, financial gain, or aggrandizement. We should treat a Christian story like a piece of music, or a historical claim, or a hypothesis in science—one that needs to be tested not musically, historically, or scientifically, but relationally. Obviously, religious stories, like music, are not judged by precise scientific experiments. But there is still evidence. There is evidence of failed stories from the lives of slaves, feminists, blacks, Jews, women accused of witchcraft, gays, children, heretics, heathen, and more.

With a relational test, many Christian stories can simply be dismissed because they fail to promote relational wholeness or don't comport with reality as we know it today. Many interpretations of the Bible and theological statements are based on outdated philosophical, scientific, and theological categories, and thus make little sense today. More theology can be dismissed because it is just a hotbed of nastiness. The relational test says that one cannot be right in one's thinking if it leads to treating others poorly. The relational test helps narrow down the number of useful stories. We cannot build until we have removed the rubble.

Incidentally, this differs from what Christians normally have as tests. Denominations and churches have their tests but usually center on whether you have the correct "belief." Want to become a member of a church? Are you Catholic? Are you evangelical? Do you believe Jesus died for your sins? Do you believe in believer's baptism? Or if you want to become a Presbyterian pastor, the criteria may be your adherence to the Westminster Confession of Faith, or if Lutheran, the Formula of Concord, or if Anglican, the Thirty-nine Articles of Religion, or if Methodist, the works of John Wesley.

In summary, a relational test looks for evidence from Christians:

- Evidence that they live in the twenty-first century and thus accept reality as we know it today.

- Evidence that their stories stress the central gospel themes of love, freedom, incarnation, and equality; that their stories embody the many examples of Jesus, including the outcast; that their stories exemplify the central parables of the gospel, which stress *compassion* and that there are in fact *good* people who are outside their group.

- Evidence that their stories are not hindering transformation because they are trapped in the morality and mindset of the ancient past.

- Evidence that their stories are not isolated, self-referential musings that only titillate a few like-minded people and serve no use for the world.
- Evidence that they are helping with the decline of violence, promoting reconciliation, being kind to the outsider, and being generous to those with whom they disagree.
- Evidence that the stories Christians tell are for all humans, for example, giving women and LGBTQ people full rights and dignity; stories that protect children; stories that include minorities.
- Evidence that they are promoting healthy relationships with the environment.
- Evidence—because without evidence, morals can be anything you choose from the Bible. And these morals cannot be corrected or challenged because it's God's word. It should be clear by now that people can derive any morality from the Bible. Want to subjugate women? There are texts for you, a tradition to follow, or a priest to listen to—never mind the considerable evidence of harmful outcomes for women and society.

Jonah's dilemma (Is faith a virtue?)

Forty seminary students at Princeton Theological Seminary waited anxiously to deliver a sermon upon which they were to be graded.[154] Half were given the Parable of the Good Samaritan to preach on. The others covered different topics. But they were unaware that they were part of a larger experiment. Just before they had to preach, they had to cross an alleyway where a man was slumped, coughing, and moaning in pain. Of the forty students, only sixteen (40 percent) offered some help. Some even stepped over the man to get to their building. The result of the experiment: those preaching on the Good Samaritan did not statistically stop more than those who preached on something else. Studying and talking about the Good Samaritan did not increase caring behavior.

Even after weeding out rotten stories, we need something more than simply telling wonderful stories. It is one thing to preach on the parable of the Good Samaritan and elevate it as an example and goal; it is another thing to help the person who everyone else ignores. In other words, it is one thing to affirm an excellent story; it is another to live it. It is the difference between faith and faithfulness.

Many biblical stories address this problem—that people claim a "faith" adherence, but their actions tell another story. For example, in the famous story of Jonah, Jonah provides one of the better descriptions of God in the Hebrew Bible: that God is gracious and merciful, slow to anger, abounding in love, and relents from sending judgment (Jonah 4:2). God sent Jonah on a mission to speak to the Ninevites about their wickedness. As we know, Jonah first refuses to talk with his enemies, ends up on a boat, and hightails it in the opposite direction. A storm and a great fish put an end to that escapade, and Jonah ends up preaching to the Ninevites. The Ninevites promptly repent, God doesn't send his threatened destruction, and Jonah is left fuming. At this point, Jonah gives that declaration about the character of God. It is his faith statement, but at every point, Jonah's character is the opposite. Jonah is ungracious, quick to anger, unloving, and desires swift judgment. Jonah waxes poetic about the love of God, while refusing to love those outside his tribe.

The story calls for faithfulness rather than faith statements; it does not stress faith, but being *faithful*. This is one reason I didn't include "faith" in the relational test. Professions of faith are not evidence of a worthwhile life. In fact, "faith" can be an enemy of accepting reality, of pursuing transformation, of widening relationships. "I'll *believe* this no matter how compelling contrary evidence may be"; or "My 'faith' makes me superior and in opposition to you"; or a faith as the bumper sticker says, "The Bible says it, I believe it, that settles it."

The Devil's Dictionary defines faith as "belief without evidence in what is told by one who speaks without knowledge, of things without parallel."[155] This sums up the negative portrayal that many have about "faith." One criticism against faith is that it has little self-correction, few checks and balances, and often strengthens in the face of contrary evidence. It doesn't help matters when we read Kierkegaard saying, "Christian faith requires that faith persists in the face of the impossible." This view of faith can make people sound like they are living in Wonderland: "I've believed as many as six impossible things before breakfast."[156]

Christopher Hitchens thought that out of all the virtues, faith is the most overrated. Is faith even a virtue? Is "faith" belief without evidence? Is it a leap into the dark? Is it kissing goodbye to reason and common sense? It can be. Some perspectives on faith include:

- Faith as magic. Never mind medicine, if you just have faith, your child will be healed. Or, if you have faith you may handle snakes and not get bitten. Or, you are still sick because you don't have enough faith.

- Faith as mystery. Belief in the great unknown and unknowable. I don't understand this; this makes no sense, but I'm going to believe anyway. Although I don't know the answers, God as the ultimate mystery must know the answer.
- Faith as a get-out-of-jail free card, an excuse for behavior. No matter how bad you are, if you have faith, you will be saved.
- Faith as a belief in a set of doctrines. An affirmation of what one believes, such as the Apostle's Creed or Westminster Confession of Faith.
- Faith as trust in God. If you believe in Jesus, you will be saved. I trust God loves me and will take care of me.
- Faith as assurance of things unseen. Faith that I have an immaterial soul and that heaven is real.

Some views are more harmful than others. Faith as magic is obviously problematic and often deadly. Faith as a belief in a set of doctrines often ends up with people believing ideas that no longer have any currency today—holding "truths" that are fossilized remains of long-gone creatures who once lived in a very different world. Faith as assurance of things unseen lacks concreteness and often sounds like wishful dreaming.

To expand on just one of these: faith as belief in doctrines or "truths" is often more problematic than first appears. For one, these beliefs can impede stories and deny a story's direction, development, and surprises. As such, they hinder change and growth. They close avenues to critical thought, skeptical inquiry, and progress. Often this "faith" is tied to faith in authority figures who have given their imprimatur to official teaching. This teaching, proclaimed and believed, becomes the boundary markers for the group to identify the community, and to reject those who believe other truths. People can now be as nasty and evil as they want, provided they are defending the "faith." Belief in the "truth" or "sound doctrine" is a coded message for precisely staying *out* of relationships. We can see this in the Roman Catholic child abuse scandal that by any account should have launched a substantial and lengthy period of repentance. Nevertheless, over the decades there appeared more concern expressed over dissident theology rather than abusive priests. We see this in some conservative Protestant seminaries and colleges which quickly label people as heretics and dismiss in the name of "truth" even tenured faculty members for violating the group's beliefs. "Sound doctrine" is now a vehicle to speed away from people, and too bad if you run over someone in the process. Even from the beginning of the Christian movement, Jesus is reported saying to his disciples, "They will put you out of the synagogues. Indeed, an hour is coming when those who kill you will think that by doing so they are offering worship to God" (John 16:2). Faith as doctrinal belief can be vastly more deadly than faith as magic.

New Testament scholarship in the last few decades has increasingly recognized that "faith" and "faithfulness" are extremely close. In fact, the Greek word *pistis* can be translated either "faith" or "faithfulness," and we cannot make a sharp distinction between the two. Debates have thus occurred over whether passages in the New Testament should be translated "faith in Jesus Christ" or "the faithfulness of Jesus Christ." For the more linguistically minded, it is whether the Greek construction is an objective or subjective genitive. In passages such as Romans 3:21–22 and Galatians 2:16, scholarship leans toward the second, so that Romans 3:21–22 should read the "righteousness of God is revealed through the faithfulness of Jesus," and not "the righteousness of God through faith in Jesus Christ." For some people, the difference is a big deal. Is Paul saying that the righteousness of God is revealed through the faithfulness of Jesus; or is the righteousness of God revealed through a person's faith in Jesus? The point for our purposes is that faith and faithfulness are inseparably joined.

The apostle Paul closely connected faith and faithfulness. Paul famously began and ended his letter to the Romans with the phrase "the obedience of faith." And what is Paul's answer to relational failure, for example, the "biting and devouring" (Gal 5:15) going on at the Jurassic church of Galatia? For Paul, the only thing that matters is faith that expresses itself in love (Gal 5:6). For Paul, the life he leads he lives by the faithfulness of the Son of God (Gal 2:20) and for him this is living by the Spirit, which manifests all the fruit of the Spirit, such as love, patience, and kindness.

Like redefining sin as relational failure, we can define faith in relational categories, and this serves as another example of where Christian stories can transform.

Christians could give "faith" a more "faithful" emphasis. This would remain connected to New Testament narratives, while emphasizing faithfulness in relationships—especially toward women, minorities, LGBTQ, and being faithful in our social contracts. The word "faithful" has more traction, in that it can include the idea of being trustworthy, that the games we play are played with honesty, clarity, loyalty, and start with trust. Being faithful is being loving, honest, and loyal. Faithfulness opens the conversation. Instead of faith being committed to a parochial ideology, faithfulness involves listening—listening to the oppressed, the marginalized, the abused, the outsider, and the forgotten.

Faith is a virtue when it is faithfulness. Truth and faith, viewed relationally, are relating truthfully and faithfully to others.

Granted people will still have their beliefs, but beliefs should be recognized for what they are. In speaking about reality, stories, and beliefs, there is a hierarchy: reality trumps stories, and stories trump beliefs.

A wonderful story is told about one of the world's most beautiful, admired, and coveted musical instruments—the Stradivarius violin. What was Antonio Stradivari's (1644–1737) secret that some 350 years ago he created instruments that now sell for millions of dollars and are played in the world's finest orchestras? By what alchemy had this magician from Cremona transformed humble wood into an instrument worth far more than its weight in gold? All kinds of theories have been proposed, each one adding to the myth. Did Stradivari have some secret method that has been long lost? Were there special ingredients involved? Did he use a special varnish? Perhaps there were secret chemicals used to treat the wood for fungus and worms. Was it the glue he used, or unknown wood preservatives? Perhaps there was a darker secret, as portrayed in the film *Red Violin*, where the violin maker used human blood in his varnish.[157] Who knows, perhaps Stradivari found some dragon's blood. Or was it the Little Ice Age that swept across Europe in 1550–1850, slowing the growth of trees, causing the rings in trees to be tighter, and thus producing a denser wood? Whatever his secret, no one has discovered it or reproduced his masterpieces. It is a wonderful story with a romantic feel—that a genius in ages past had something that we have now lost with our science, technology, and mass production.

But the story is most probably incorrect. For one thing, a Stradivarius today is not the same instrument created by Antonio. They have undergone all kinds of repairs and modifications. The instruments of his time could not generate enough volume for a modern orchestra. Bridges, necks, fingerboards, and strings have all been adjusted, modified, or replaced. Along with various other repairs, it is now a different instrument. In addition, blind tests (where the audience doesn't know what violin is being played) and double-blind experiments (where neither the audience nor the player know what instrument is being used) have been conducted. The results? Players and audience cannot tell the difference between a Stradivarius and a $10,000 modern violin.[158] It's a pity. I really liked the story. Writers are reminded to murder their darlings—that seemingly brilliant piece of writing that you desperately try to squeeze in—kill it. It doesn't fit or work. Same with our stories. Sometimes we must murder our darlings. I liked the story of the exceptional value of a Stradivarius, just as I consider a Concert D Hamburg Steinway to be the pinnacle of piano creation. And yes, it differs from a New York Steinway, and no, I don't want to be subjected to a blind test!

Beliefs are abstractions from stories, and stories are abstractions from reality. In other words, beliefs are not reality. Beliefs are transient abstractions, attempts to codify a story. They are even further removed from reality than stories, although they are often not thought of that way. Religious beliefs are usually accorded the place of reality and thus provide fertile soil for conflict. The conflicts of widely differing beliefs within Christianity are conflicts between different abstractions from different stories. Beliefs often lead to violent clashes because they are elevated to ultimate truth, because they place boundaries on thinking, because they are often immune to critique, because they are often attempts to tame and control the story for power over others. And it is a quick step from having the "truth" to violently imposing it on others. Even in the Christian story, Jesus of Nazareth meets his horrible end for the charge of blasphemy.

The best we have are stories. As Joseph Campbell said, "Mythology is the penultimate truth—penultimate because the ultimate cannot be put into words."[159] Stories are the preeminent explanations that we have in this universe, the metaphors that point to this reality, the meaningful narratives that are abstractions of reality. For example, science considered as storytelling is selecting out instances and events, against a totality, and reducing them to create a predictable and useful way of understanding things. Granted, it uses a very stringent process in order to be as useful as possible. And as our tools get better, our stories can become more complex. Now we have artificial intelligence to automate science and extend this complexity—computer programs that derive mathematical proofs, make discoveries (from biology to astronomy), and extend our minds, ears, eyes, and bodies.

Because reality is greater than stories, we should be open to adapting our stories to our unfolding understanding of the universe. Because stories are greater than belief, the religious should be far more interested in the question, "What stories do we live by?" rather than "What do we believe?" Far more important than beliefs are the transforming narratives that guide us towards a life worth living.

Chapter 5

Insiders and Outsiders: A Just Life

> As is a tale, so is life: not how long it is,
> but how good it is, is what matters.
>
> —Seneca

> There's only one rule that I know of, babies—
> God damn it, you've got to be kind.
>
> —Kurt Vonnegut

> The good life is one inspired by love
> and guided by knowledge.
>
> —Bertrand Russell

The gods must be crazy

THE SIGNIFICANT OBSTACLE TO the quest for the life worth living is the problem of "insiders versus outsiders." Here one group wins and the other loses; where zero-sum, finite games deprive whole groups of people from living worthwhile lives. Xenophobia, misogyny, and racism are examples of this insider-outsider mentality. So are the injustices between poor and wealthy, female and male, black and white, gay and straight. Likewise, violence between groups and wars between nations thrives on inciting an insider-outsider mindset. Extreme nationalism, dangerous right-wing movements, foreign and domestic terrorist groups, and radical religious groups are other examples. We can also place environmental exploitation in this category, where one group of humans ruin the environment to the detriment of other living beings.

In keeping with my aim of interacting with Christianity, the question arises: Overall, does Christianity help or hinder overcoming this "insider-outsider" barrier to the good life? (The question could obviously be asked of other religious or secular groups.) We are aware of toxic forms of Christianity that promote social discord, but do even the more enlightened versions of Christianity encourage an unhealthy division between people? And if so, can they ever overcome this insider-outsider rift? Progressive Christians can and have altered their views, for example, on the atonement, creation, evolution, women, slavery, or hell. But is the problem of insiders versus outsiders an insurmountable hurdle for even the better forms of Christianity?

A 2011 Barna study, conducted over five years, found six reasons young people are leaving the church.[160] To summarize these six areas: (1) Churches are overprotective and can demonize things outside the church; (2) Churches are shallow and irrelevant; (3) Churches are anti-science; (4) Churches' teaching on sexuality are simplistic and judgmental; (5) The exclusive claims of Christianity; (6) Churches don't help with intellectual questions and don't help people when they have doubts about whether Christianity makes sense.

These reasons are not from people outside (from those who have never associated with the church) but from teenagers who were once regular church attenders and then left.

Many of these reasons arise from what we may place under our rubric of "insiders versus outsiders." Enormous societal pressures outside Christianity challenge churches both intellectually and ethically. We have scientific stories challenging Christian stories. We have psychology presenting insightful models for understanding human behavior and relationships. We have secular humanism arguing that it has better ideas for human living and flourishing. We have the feminist and LGBTQ communities challenging Christian views on human rights, morality, sex, and gender. We have other religions that must be accounted for—and in a pluralistic and interconnected world, these religions are increasingly difficult to ignore or demonize. We even have outsiders who sometimes want to marry those inside the church!

Against such challenges are the exclusive claims of Christianity. In Christian stories there is an exclusiveness that creates and promotes an insider-outsider problem. Many are firm and sure that Jesus is the way, the truth, the life, and no one comes to God except through Jesus. Those outside our group need salvation. They need our help, but we can survive without theirs. Many believe that other religions arise because of idolatry or demonic influences. Many, following Paul, say that there is nothing in common between a believer and unbeliever, that there is no agreement between Christ and Beliar, and thus emphasize the importance of marrying only other Christians (2 Cor 6:15). Christians give plenty of arguments why gays are sinners and should remain outside their group. One cannot be a minister, pastor, or priest in most Christian denominations if you are (overtly) gay. In Christian colleges or seminaries, you usually cannot teach without agreeing to an exclusive statement of faith. In fact, you usually cannot be a student either—most require a testimonial to show that you are part of the in-group.

Doctrines such as the inerrancy of Scripture or the infallibility of the pope are exclusive claims that further cement differences between groups. God has revealed everything to us. We are right and without error, or, at least, we have access to the inerrant truth. There are doctrines among Calvinists such as double predestination where God predestined before the foundation of the world those who would believe in God, a view that excludes a vast majority. And there is the doctrine of "limited atonement," which is not called "limited" for nothing. Jesus died only for those who were predestined—the elect, the chosen. And within conservative coalitions, we have the ultimate outsider belief—hell. This belief has terrorized and tormented people for eons, where those who are not part of the group are believed to await eternal torture. Even those inside the group sometimes suffer from a kind of Stockholm syndrome—from being showered with kindness (God loves you) and terror (hell awaits if you defect) in equal doses.

This insider-outsider exclusiveness also finds expression within and between Christian groups. Even among themselves there is no unity or inclusiveness. The title "antichrist" can be assigned to Hillary Clinton, Donald Trump, or a pope. Many churches, denominations, and seminaries perpetrate an exclusive and insular mindset even within themselves. To join us, you need to be pre-millennial, or Methodist, or Trinitarian, or believe in adult baptism, or penal substitution, or transubstantiation, or hold to the five points of Calvinism (four is unacceptable). To be part of our group, you must accept the Book of Common Prayer, or speak in tongues, or believe that only men can be pastors, or hold to a six-day creation view, or the immaculate conception of Mary, or disavow gay marriage. The list is endless. Viewed from the outside, the message is, "If you want to be part of our community, become like us." Borg-like, we'll assimilate your distinctives into our collective.

Many denominations, churches, and seminaries have a tiring propensity to exclude and set their group against another. Many define themselves by whom they oppose and why—usually some doctrinal difference—and this exclusion breeds further hostility and contempt. There are heretics within and heathen without. I once tried to move from being an ordained pastor in one Presbyterian denomination to another Presbyterian denomination—a process that I thought would only require signing some paperwork. But because these two denominations dislike each other, I was told I would have to do all the ordination exams again—including comprehensive exams on Greek, Hebrew, the Bible, and church history. I declined. Just look at a chart illustrating the history of Presbyterian churches in the United States—with all their divisions and splits. Think of a map of the London Underground and you will get the general idea. Apparently, Presbyterians don't like other Presbyterians.

Many churches lagged and often supported exclusion when it came to human rights for slaves, women, blacks, African Americans, and the LGBTQ community. This dismal behavior is often accompanied by a blindness to this exclusion. William Temple, former archbishop of Canterbury, once said, "The church is the only society in the world that exists for the benefit of those who are not its members." This is certainly prescriptive and not descriptive, an aspirational statement of what the church should be. Missionaries who travel to foreign lands, ostensibly for the benefit of others, often repeat Temple's statement. But there is a crucial relational flaw in that the ultimate goal of missionary work is to bring outsiders into the missionaries' coalition, usually by convincing them that they are misguided, lost sinners, and that the missionaries possess the truth and failure to accept and follow it will have the direst consequences, lasting for eternity.

From the outside, Sam Harris describes how many people see the church, noting, "The history of Christianity is principally a story of mankind's misery and ignorance rather than of its requited love of God."[161] Will churches and Christians undergo the necessary self-examination by looking at themselves through the eyes of others?

The exclusive claims of Christianity are a significant reason even people who used to attend church have left. Churches are becoming increasingly concerned about the younger generation who have exited the church in significant numbers—the "dones" who are fed up with Christianity, and those who now self-identify as "nones," as having no religious affiliation.

The bio-cultural study of religion

There is an additional area, yet unmentioned, that presents another considerable intellectual challenge to Christianity and its stories—the bio-cultural study of religion, which gives plausible reasons how religions evolve and why they are so susceptible to insider-outsider problems. As we will see, these studies raise the question whether Christian stories will face dissolution as they attempt to overcome the insider-outsider problem.

LeRon Shults, professor of theology and philosophy at the University of Agder, Norway, summarizes the findings from the bio-cultural study of religion—findings that incorporate a vast field of research, including "archeology, cognitive science, evolutionary neurobiology, moral psychology, social anthropology, and political theory."[162] Shults argues that just as we have plausible explanations where babies come from, we now also have plausible explanations for how and why gods are born. And depending on the audience, both conversations can be uncomfortable but necessary. Shults writes:

> In the early ancestral environment the selective advantage went to hominids whose cognitive capacities enabled them to quickly *detect* relevant agents (such as predators, prey, and partners) in the natural environment, and whose groups were adequately *protected* from the dissolution that could result from too many defectors and cheaters in the social environment.
>
> Hyper-sensitive detection often led to false positives, e.g., identifying a noise in the forest as a predator (or prey) when it was really the wind. However, occasionally it really was a predator (or prey) and those whose detective capacities were weak or lazy—it's probably just the wind—got eaten (or failed to eat) and so their genes were not passed on. Hyper-sensitive protection often led to serious punishment of cheaters, the demand for costly signals of commitment from those suspected of considering defection, and willingness to attack and kill members of out-groups. The good news (for the in-group) is that these strategies did in fact lead to stronger (longer-lasting) coalitions.
>
> In fact, *over*-sensitive detection and protection (and other components of anthropomorphic promiscuity and sociographic prudery) increased the chance of survival during a critical period of time in human history. In earlier chapters, we reviewed part of the growing body of evidence that suggests that around 90,000–70,000 years ago, some *Homo sapiens* groups developed more complex beliefs and rituals in which they imaginatively engaged supernatural agents they detected in the environment (e.g., spirits attributed responsibility for weather, good hunting, etc.). These contingently embodied (or ontologically confused) intentional forces were often believed to have the power to punish cheaters or defectors (or their family members). They also might be watching at any time, which increased group member's motivation to follow social norms.

Sometime around 60,000 years ago it appears that some of these "god bearing" groups left Africa, out-competing all other hominid species and spreading out across the Levant and into Europe and Asia, eventually incorporating other kinds of supernatural agents such as ancestor ghosts.[163]

How did humans with their "hyperactive agency detector" jump to positing disembodied or supernatural agents? David Lewis-Williams, professor of cognitive archeology at the University of the Witwatersrand, South Africa, for example, has argued that this jump can be understood from altered states of consciousness, states that can be achieved through various methods, such as sleep deprivation, hunger, intense dancing, meditation, extreme pain, schizophrenia, or hallucinogenic plants.[164] Whether through altered states of consciousness, dreams, hallucinations of dead loved ones, or the vivid imaginations of children,[165] the jump was made, and humans mistook these images for a supernatural realm. And gods were born.

As time passed and as communities grew, bigger gods were necessary to sustain bigger groups, until we reach the creation of an infinite God whose realm and reach encompasses all groups, and he watches over all. Infinity, applied to God, however, introduced other difficulties.[166] How can one have an infinite God who encompasses all finite beings who are separate? With infinity now applied to every attribute of God—all-knowing, all-loving, all-powerful—arises the unsolvable problem of evil and suffering. Widespread evil and suffering exists, but it shouldn't if there is One who knows about it, who is loving, and who has the power to do something about it.

From our evolutionary past, we have inherited two overactive processes: hypersensitive detection and hypersensitive protection. These mechanisms once enabled our ancestors to survive. Thus, we see faces on Mars, rabbits in the clouds, Jesus on a piece of toast, and ghostly apparitions in photographs. We are also overprotective of our group, and the gods aid this protection. Gods who watch over the coalition have helped keep everyone in check because the group believes that their god can spot cheaters, punish miscreants, and encourage exemplary behavior. Thus, we give birth to gods and keep them around, developing rituals with smells and bells to reinforce these beliefs, and adding costly signaling to show faithfulness to the group, such as giving 10 percent of one's salary, attending long prayer meetings, or affirming some crazy belief. These all add to the ongoing detection and protection of the gods. The problem, however, is that although this strengthens the coalition, it also alienates the group from outsiders and creates a hostile us-versus-them attitude that can spiral into violence. What once helped our survival when we lived in small groups is now increasingly problematic and sometimes lethal in our modern interconnected world.

From the bio-cultural study of religion, we now have plausible and probable explanations for how gods are born and why we keep them around. Having supernatural agents strengthens that particular community but has the side effect of strengthening an insider-outsider mentality. With our gods, our beliefs, culture, values, and behavior are given a transcendent basis and origin. Outsiders are therefore often wrong, inferior, impure, or evil.

* * *

There is, however, in the New Testament, an inbuilt critique of the insider-outsider problem. There are resources within Christian stories that go at least some distance necessary to promote better relationships with outsiders. We have already mentioned abolitionists and feminists who found themes of love and freedom resonating with their concerns, and who emphasized passages such as Galatians 3:28—sometimes called the Magna Carta of Christianity—that in Christ there are no divisions, no longer Jew or Greek, slave or free, male or female. We saw that Paul and the early church argued for including the gentiles, even though their Scriptures were exclusive. We have mentioned Jesus' parables, including the Good Samaritan, which emphasizes that the *good* person in this case was an outsider. Most "outsiders" are out precisely because they are considered not-good and not-right. But in the Good Samaritan, the good outsider outdoes everyone in terms of compassion and love.

In fact, many stories of Jesus tell of his love for outsiders—for people on the fringes of society, for people whom society shuns and excludes. For instance, when parents bring their children to Jesus, and the disciples try to shoo them away, we read, "But Jesus called for them and said, 'Let the little children come to me, and do not stop them; for it is to such as these that the kingdom of God belongs'" (Luke 18:16). Jesus turns the table by telling adults (in this case, his disciples) that they must become like the people they exclude. On another occasion, Jesus says to some Israelites regarding a gentile, "I tell you, not even in Israel have I found such faith" (Luke 7:9). Again, Jesus praises the excluded (a gentile Roman soldier) and encourages Israel to model their faith on this outsider. And as to his friends, Jesus didn't choose any disciples from the in-crowd. Jesus reserved his harshest language for insiders, and he repeatedly hung out with outsiders, earning him the title "friend of sinners and tax collectors."

If there was one thing that riled up people, it was Jesus' relationship with outsiders. In Luke 4:14–22, we read that everyone was amazed at his teaching and everyone spoke well of him. But then Jesus spoke of God's concern for the outsider with two examples. (1) In the time of Elijah, when a great famine gripped the land, Elijah was not sent to the many widows in Israel but to the widow at Zarephath in Sidon. And (2) in the time of Elisha, he was not sent to heal the many lepers in Israel but to Naaman the Syrian. The result? "When they heard this, all in the synagogue were filled with rage. They got up, drove him out of the town, and led him to the brow of the hill on which their town was built, so that they might hurl him off the cliff" (Luke 4:28–29). There are other examples. Jesus had the gall to make these outsiders the heroes in his stories. In Luke 18:9–14, Jesus tells the Parable of the Pharisee and the Tax Collector, and Jesus makes the tax collector the hero of the story. The righteous one in that society is not right before God, but the unrighteous one is.

A cartoon once had Jesus giving the Sermon on the Mount and saying, "Now break up into sects and try to kill each other." Some tragic humor, for in the Sermon on the Mount the key relational test is how you treat the outsider: "For if you love those who love you, what reward do you have? Do not even the tax collectors do the same? And if you greet only your brothers and sisters, what more are you doing than others? Do not even the gentiles do the same?" (Matt 5:46–47).

Of course, I'm highlighting particular passages and ignoring others. Like abolitionists or Christian feminists, I'm elevating some stories above others and interpreting these stories in a relational way. Even as we have discussed the central figure of Jesus I have not, for example, highlighted Jesus' violent actions in the temple, or his instruction to gouge out an eye for having a lustful thought, or to hate and leave your family for him, or that he chose twelve *male* disciples, or didn't condemn the institution of slavery, or his prohibition against marrying a divorced woman, or his violent teachings on the end times, hell, torture, and judgment—where, for example, those who showed no compassion on earth, are absurdly showed no compassion on judgement day—and sent to eternal fire and punishment.

Given that the insider-outsider problem is so prevalent and ingrained in churches and denominations, if Christianity is to promote the life worth living, it will have to downplay stories that flame division and elevate those stories that go some distance in addressing relationships with outsiders.

Christians, for example, may elevate the famous story of Jesus' conversation with a Samaritan woman—a woman excluded for three main reasons: her race, sex, and morals. She is a Samaritan, a woman, and one who has gone through five husbands and the person she is living with is not her husband. One strike would be enough to show you the door, three strikes would get you a swift boot on your way out. There were plenty of reasons to exclude Samaritans. They were the wrong race. They have the wrong Bible, the wrong view of the temple, and the wrong theology. Yet Jesus listens and engages in dialogue.

Or as another example, Christians may elevate the stories of Jesus socializing with tax collectors. A recurring phrase in the New Testament is "sinners and tax collectors." Not only are tax collectors lumped together with "sinners," but also they are the one group of people singled out and identified as being rotten.

Tax collectors are no different in principle from any who collaborate in the oppression of their own people, at the behest of others, to advance their personal interests. These include the Jewish kapos in the death camps, the Vichy French, the Norwegian Quisling government, black South African policemen during apartheid, and any number of spies and informants in the USSR satellites. It stretches the bounds of human acceptance to a breaking point to relieve these individuals of the responsibility for and consequences of their own decisions and malicious actions. No wonder Dante reserved the innermost circle of hell for betrayers.

Yet, Jesus socializes with tax collectors, including choosing one to be his disciple (Matthew the tax collector in Matthew 9:9–13) and calling another a child of Abraham (Zacchaeus in Luke 19:1–10). The attraction was mutual. Tax collectors came to hear Jesus speak and Jesus ate and drank with them, to such a degree that Jesus' enemies called him a "friend of sinners and tax collectors" (Matt 11:19; Luke 15:1–2). Jesus prefers dinner parties with the scum of the earth. He prefers their company in contrast to the religious insiders, who quickly made Jesus an outsider, declaring him not-kosher.

In today's world, depending on the specific society, these "tax collectors" could be a wide variety of people—people of color, females, traitors, untouchables, prostitutes, illegal aliens, or LGBTQ people.

Exclusive clubs: the secret requirement for membership

If we want to exclude, we can find any reason. The reasons for exclusion can be anything: a person's class, race, sex, physical features, theology, religion, clothes, interests, morals, political views, sexual orientation, education, lifestyle, car, or way of talking. We can exclude someone to control their behavior—until they shape up, tidy up, or wake up. We can exclude others because we fear intimacy. We can exclude people when we think they are making us look bad. We can exclude other groups to further our own coalition that provides us access to money, power over others, status, and other resources. In fact, if we are looking for a reason to exclude, there is always one available, no matter how small. Freud spoke about the "narcissism of the small difference." Often it is the smallest difference that is the basis for hostility and exclusion, hence the joke that the reason academic debates can be so acrimonious is because the stakes are so small.

Of course, many exclusive relationships are good and valuable. Many groups are innocuous and are simply people with shared ideas, values, stories, interests, and culture. Marriages, parent-child relationships, siblings, close friends, all have their exclusivity. We lack the ability and time to include everyone in our relational sphere of influence. We can handle a few intimate relationships, some good friends, and several acquaintances. Our original hunter-gatherer groupings and consequent evolution limits our meaningful engagement to a few people. The Dunbar number suggests that the number of social relationships we can sustain is around 150, never mind what Facebook says. In choosing some relationships, we exclude others. And we rightly protect these relationships.

The problem arises with *over*protection, where our hypersensitive protection mechanisms run rampant. This is our human default; thus, the challenge is to be consciously aware of our hypersensitivity mechanisms and not react to them mindlessly. Of concern is an exclusive mentality that leads to shunning, meanness, contempt, oppression, violence, and even murder, where humans violently exclude others, ruin their chances for worthwhile lives, and squander resources for those outside their group. Of concern are groups whose identity, worth, conduct, and myth of superiority are energized by excluding others.

The official membership requirements for these types of exclusive clubs are varied, some costing hundreds of thousands of dollars. Or a strictly-held theological position, precisely and rigorously spelled out in a theological tome, will gain admittance. Or contempt for Muslims, or Jews, or Christians, or Iranians, or Tutsis, or atheists will get one in. But no matter how varied these outward requirements, concealed is one essential requirement for these exclusive clubs, a requirement that is *never* listed as a requirement, and that is *pretense*—a hypocrisy that is the bane of all malignant exclusive coalitions.

To illustrate my point, there is a passage in the New Testament where we find a critique of pretense, the primary requirement of nasty exclusive clubs. This passage also serves as one final example of a New Testament critique against an insider-outsider mentality. In Luke 11:37–52 we find an extensive interaction between Jesus and religious leaders. For clarity, I'll include the passage:

> While he [Jesus] was speaking, a Pharisee invited him to dine with him; so he went in and took his place at the table. The Pharisee was amazed to see that he did not first wash before dinner. Then the Lord said to him, "Now you Pharisees clean the outside of the cup and of the dish, but inside you are full of greed and wickedness. You fools! Did not the one who made the outside make the inside also? So give for alms those things that are within; and see, everything will be clean for you.
>
> "But woe to you Pharisees! For you tithe mint and rue and herbs of all kinds, and neglect justice and the love of God; it is these you ought to have practiced, without neglecting the others. Woe to you Pharisees! For you love to have the seat of honor in the synagogues and to be greeted with respect in the marketplaces. Woe to you! For you are like unmarked graves, and people walk over them without realizing it."
>
> One of the lawyers answered him, "Teacher, when you say these things, you insult us too." And he said, "Woe also to you lawyers! For you load people with burdens hard to bear, and you yourselves do not lift a finger to ease them. Woe to you! For you build the tombs of the prophets whom your ancestors killed. So you are witnesses and approve of the deeds of your ancestors; for they killed them, and you build their tombs. Therefore also the Wisdom of God said, 'I will send them prophets and apostles, some of whom they will kill and persecute,' so that this generation may be charged with the blood of all the prophets shed since the foundation of the world, from the blood of Abel to the blood of Zechariah, who perished between the altar and the sanctuary. Yes, I tell you, it will be charged against this generation. Woe to you lawyers! For you have taken away the key of knowledge; you did not enter yourselves, and you hindered those who were entering."

Here Jesus addresses a significant problem with exclusive clubs—pretense. He accuses the religious leaders of cleaning the outside and neglecting the mess inside (Although, historically the Pharisees were not these horrible people as so often described in the New Testament). Instead of a virtuous character producing a good life, they thought the opposite—that if we pretend to live a good life, it will work inwardly. Their pretense is further seen when Jesus says they love the greetings in the marketplace and the important seats in the synagogue—the seats upfront in prominent view where everyone can see how important they are, and the greetings where everyone calls them Rabbi (Reverend, Professor, Pastor, Doctor, or whatever). The desire for recognition, respect, and power is based on pretense—a belief that one deserves this praise and honor.

This way of living has a corrupting influence. Jesus calls them "unmarked graves." In that time, if you touched a grave, the Mosaic law stated that you were unclean for seven days (Num 19:16). While graves were usually placed outside towns and sometimes inconspicuous tombs were whitewashed to warn travelers, there could be a problem, however, if you walked over an unmarked grave and were defiled without knowing it. Jesus compares the religious leaders to these hidden graves. They are the ones who were defiling people, and the people were unaware. A life of pretense contains a hidden danger, something hard to see, an elusive evil.

Pretense is hard to recognize because it often looks good on the outside and relates to appearances, reputation, and self-righteousness. Although, every now again, it appears for all to see. Pretense comes with a cloaking device, like a Klingon warbird in the Star Trek universe—a massive battleship geared with an impressive ability to render itself almost invisible. In *Star Trek*, finding Klingon warships is notoriously difficult. While searching space, you may see only a slight shimmering disturbance, but nothing that you can detect by the usual tracking methods—until the vessel decloaks and blasts you. Likewise, pretense is a disturbance in the relational continuum, hard to nail down and detect, until it attacks, and then for a moment you see the reality.

But didn't these religious leaders build tombs for the prophets, and doesn't that show their upright lives? Again, it is pretense. This was just another outward ploy to impress people by pretending to honor the revered prophets. Jesus rebukes them on this point as well. Jesus holds these religious leaders accountable for the deaths of the all the prophets from Abel to Zechariah. Following the book order of the Hebrew Bible, Genesis is first with Abel's death and 2 Chronicles is the last book, with Zechariah's death mentioned at the end in 2 Chronicles chapter 24, representing the first and last murders in the Hebrew Bible. In other words, Jesus says to the teachers of the law, "You would have killed them all—from Abel to Zechariah—because all of them testified against your way of life." The proverb warns, "Dead men tell no tales." The religious leaders professed to honor the memory of the prophets, yet they lived the same lifestyle that the prophets preached against. It's a pity that "every society honors its live conformists and its dead troublemakers," per Mignon McLaughlin.[167] Why pay homage to the dead if you can't stand the living?

Nasty exclusive clubs thrive on pretense. The only way to be "better" and more "exclusive" than others is to pretend—pretend that in some fashion we are better than others. Pretend that we are not in the common boat of humanity and live a lie. On the back of every membership card of these exclusive clubs should be the word "pretend." Join us, pretend, and bring all available means to prop up this pretense—revising of memories, history, culture, literature, and deeds. Pretend that men are superior to women, free superior to slaves, rich superior to poor, Serbs to Croats, CEOs to workers, white South Africans to blacks, Americans to Iranians, Christians to atheists. Pretense is a common denominator and lays the foundation for these exclusive clubs. All racist and sexist ideas are built on myth, lies, and pretense. And especially if you want to start a war, you'll need heaps of pretense and pretexts to convince people and to justify your actions.

Pretense is self-deception, a convenient ignorance, a flight from reality, from which develops all manner of exclusion—thus hindering the life worth living. Pretense fails a relational test, for pretense is being out of touch (relationship) with reality. Pretense is a cognitive bias that creates its own reality, where people convince themselves of the truth of their views despite a mass of contradictory evidence. Jesus concludes his rebuke by saying this way of life places onerous burdens on people, takes away the key to knowledge, and hinders others from gaining wisdom. There is most probably a relational law that says the more exclusive the group, the more pretense is needed to establish and maintain the group, and thus the more self-righteous, immoral, and isolated it becomes. This increasing isolation further insulates the club from disruption and listening to feedback from the outside.

The seeds of dissolution

Several stories in the New Testament condemn harmful insider-outsider dynamics. In emphasizing these stories, however, we should note that there are other passages in the New Testament that promote exclusivity—stories that have been used to oppress and create conflict with many, including slaves, women, LGBTQ people, atheists, Christians in different denominations, and other religious believers. We have seen how Christianity is a multitudinous mass of stories, but that even in this mass we can highlight and bring to the foreground an internal critique of insiders versus outsiders. The New Testament records the two founding figures of Christianity, Jesus and Paul, as ones who struggled to overcome the insider-outsider divide: Jesus by confronting the elite insiders, associating with tax collectors, lepers, prostitutes, and cripples, and by making outsiders heroes of stories; and Paul by including the gentiles, which took a rereading of the Hebrew Bible.

We now reach a place where we can ask: To promote the good life, how far can we push the implications of these highlighted Christian stories? We have covered some examples of Christian stories that contain a critique of insider-outsider ways of living. But we have also seen that belief in supernatural agents leads to overprotection of ingroups that results in hostility to outgroups. The result is that those outside—those who don't belong to our coalition and god—are pagan, infidels, heathen, godless, dead in sin, agents of Satan, immoral, or generally messed up. The result is a prejudice that views the "other" as inferior, immoral, and in need of help or destruction. For instance, even when people leave Christianity they are often written off as never having been "true" Christians in the first place, or that the real reason for their departure was because of immorality or a desire to engage in all kinds of depraved shenanigans. These responses are understandable, given group dynamics and the belief that supernatural agents keep everyone in check. For a group that engages in imaginative battles against evil powers and dark forces, a former Christian is an annoying outsider that needs to be written off.

Shults draws attention to two possible trajectories in theology: sacerdotal and iconoclastic.[168] This means that theology can move in god-bearing or god-dissolving directions. Because of our evolutionary heritage, the temptation is to move in the god-bearing direction. In fact, a religious coalition pressures people to restrain any flights of fancy—any theological thinking that is perceived to undermine the group. Take it too far and you are a heretic. Take it further and you are heathen. The Christian stories of inclusion and love, however, have enough substance and weight to push through these retaining walls.

Take, for example, some implications of the central Christian teaching, "God is love." Mark Noll, professor of church history at Notre Dame, in his *The Civil War as a Theological Crisis* writes about the stalemate between pro-slavery and abolitionist arguments over the Bible:

> With debate over the Bible and slavery at such a pass, and especially with the success of the pro-slavery biblical argument manifestly (if also uncomfortably) convincing to most Southerners and many in the North, difficulties abounded. The country had a problem because its most trusted religious authority, the Bible, was sounding an uncertain note. The evangelical Protestant churches had a problem because the mere fact of trusting implicitly in the Bible was not solving disagreements about what the Bible taught concerning slavery. The country and the churches were both in trouble because the remedy that finally solved the question of how to interpret the Bible was a recourse

to arms. The supreme crisis over the Bible was that there existed no apparent biblical resolution to the crisis. As I have written elsewhere, it was left to those consummate theologians, the Reverend Doctors Ulysses S. Grant and William Tecumseh Sherman, to decide what in fact the Bible actually meant.[169]

Evangelicals, some 150 years after the Civil War, still hold to the clarity, sufficiency, and authority of the Bible. Noll, an evangelical, provides an example where it was supremely important to know what the Bible taught, yet Christians reached no agreement. People found no clarity. The Bible was insufficient for the task, and it didn't speak authoritatively for either side. Abolitionists and pro-slavery supporters fought over the Bible for three decades and found no resolution. As noted before, Christians now adopt abolitionist reasoning and hermeneutics, and the pro-slavery texts in the Bible are moved to the background.

We may say that the Christian claim that "God is love" won the day. Abolitionists used the love of God (and other ideas) to override specific texts that endorsed the institution of slavery. But why stop there? Some theologians didn't and used the trajectory of the love of God to undermine other doctrines. The explanations and implications of "God loves you but will send you to hell if you defect" have kept many theologians in employment. One can sense the struggle how far to push the doctrine even in the title from the great twentieth-century theologian, Hans Urs von Balthasar's *Dare We Hope "That All Men Be Saved"? With a Short Discourse on Hell*. Many Christians rightly pushed the idea that love is absolutely incompatible and incoherent with the idea of eternally torturing someone. Eternal torture—can we ever imagine a greater evil? Some theologians concluded God would simply annihilate unbelievers rather than subject them to torture. Others argued that in the end, all people would be saved, that everyone will eventually join their group. Of course, the label "heretic" was thrown around and many objections were presented, such as that people are rotten sinners deserving punishment, that people have free will and are therefore responsible for their predicament, and don't forget about God's justice. But these have struggled to quench the flames of "God is love." And it is becoming harder. In our interconnected world, Christians now find people outside their group who are upright and good people, where it is extremely hard to say that they are rotten and deserve hell. The point, however, is that the horrific insider-outsider doctrine of hell can be swept away by the idea that "God is love."

But why stop there? We mentioned that with a God who is love and infinite, we now have the problem of evil and suffering. Widespread evil exists, yet we have a God who is infinitely loving, sees everything, and can do something about it. Each time the doctrine is pushed, there is the question whether people will move in the god-bearing or the god-dissolving direction. A god-bearing direction says, "God loves me, he saved me from the 2004 tsunami." A god-dissolving direction says, "What about the 230,000 others who were killed? Doesn't God love them as well? If a loving God is in fact present in our world, God would have at least done something."

"God is love" is like a loose string in a sweater that, when pulled enough, slowly unravels the entire garment—pro-slavery, patriarchy, homophobia, insiders and outsiders, hell, even the presence of God. So one keeps adjusting and changing Christianity, until at the end, perhaps love urges us to let everything go—conclude that these are some remarkable and imaginative stories, but that there is no supernatural agent or agents behind these stories.

The philosopher Gilles Deleuze once remarked that Christianity secretes atheism more than any other religion.[170] Perhaps this is the case, in part, because of the intractable conundrums formed from Christianity's assigning infinity to God, resulting in the problem of evil, or the problem of an infinite God encompassing all but with separate finite creatures, or other paradoxes, such as the stone paradox (Can God create a stone heavy enough that he cannot move it?). Perhaps in part this is because of a central place Christian stories give to love, truth, and relationships with outsiders. Perhaps in part this is because of the horrible history of Christianity that casts doubt on the entire enterprise.

From the biocultural study of religion, we see how supernatural agents can arise through natural evolutionary processes, and that these agents serve to protect the group to which they belong. Of course, those who don't believe in supernatural agents are not immune to insider-outsider problems. Clearly, many factors are involved in the overprotection of groups. The problem today in our increasingly interconnected world is that belief in gods leads to an overprotection of that god's group. Some Christian stories, however, have a central and sharp critique against insider-outsider thinking, but further progress beyond a certain point might well require giving up belief in supernatural agents.

Death as a way to life

Give up on God for the sake of outsiders? For Christians, this step would be giving up their lives—their worldview, their identity, their beliefs, and much of their community. Even such a drastic move, however, would find resonance in some Christian stories. Jesus himself gave up his life for others—specifically for *outsiders*. Paul's often-quoted words in the letter to the Romans say, "God proves his love for us in that while we still were sinners Christ died for us" (Rom 5:8). This sacrifice became the example for all who claim to follow Jesus. Jesus summarized what is required of those who follow him: "If any want to become my followers, let them deny themselves and take up their cross daily and follow me" (Luke 9:23). Here the pattern of Jesus' life and death becomes the exemplar or model for those who follow him. The disciples of Jesus are following someone who was crucified—not someone who had great political or religious power. After Jesus' disciples argue about who will be the greatest (Luke 22:24-27), Jesus' washes their feet—taking the lowest of occupations reserved for slaves. Everyone wants the prestigious job, but no one is in favor of cleaning the toilet. The greatest serve others. They "die" to desires for power and status. In the New Testament, there are many such examples where dying is viewed as a way to life.

The apostle Paul said of himself, "I die every day" (1 Cor 15:31). But paradoxically, he saw this reality as working life in others (2 Cor 4:11-12). Speaking of his impending death, Jesus says, "Unless a grain of wheat falls into the earth and dies, it remains just a single grain; but if it dies, it bears much fruit" (John 12:24). In fact, Jesus defines love in terms of death. "No one has greater love than this, to lay down one's life for one's friends" (John 15:13).

Death as a way to life finds resonance elsewhere. Take an example from another story we have mentioned—evolutionary theory. Here again, we find a close connection between death and life. Death and the evolutionary development of life are integrally connected. Death allows for change, development, and new life. Death gives room for others. So even as individuals die, they make room for their offspring, provide opportunities and resources for others, and allow for adaptation and novelty. Death sweeps away the old and allows for the new. Death is not only a part of life; it is a way to life. Even the elements that make up our living bodies were formed in the massive supernova death of ancient stars.

Remarkable stories encapsulate this reality of death, from the epic of Gilgamesh to Harry Potter, as they question and explore how we are to live in the light of death.

J. K. Rowling says of her Harry Potter series, "My books are largely about death."[171] It is illuminative to view the characters in her novels through the lens of how they live in light of death. Will they sacrifice their lives for others? Will they use any means possible to conquer death? Voldemort leaves a trail of death behind him as he grabs for life at any cost, abusing his supporters, overpowering and eliminating opponents, and splitting his soul into seven pieces. But in his pursuit of immortality, the very thing he fears and seeks to conquer inexorably destroys him.

Other characters, such as Lily, Harry, and Dumbledore bring life to others by giving up their lives. In doing so, they live worthwhile lives. Of course, they are imperfect, but the general direction of their lives exhibits processes of repentance and transformation. Like Dumbledore's phoenix, Fawkes, they undergo dying and rising. The opposition to Voldemort calls themselves the "Order of the Phoenix," a tribute to this way of living. For Harry to become whole, for Harry to become the master of death, for his friends to be saved, for evil to be defeated, Harry must undergo death and rebirth. In Rowling's world, death is not the worst that can happen. Thus, the stories are also about love—that love is more important than the reality of death, that love is more powerful than the reality of evil.

There are clear similarities with the overarching themes in Tolkien's The Lord of the Rings, with the arch-nemesis Sauron pouring his life into the One Ring and the heroes Sam and Frodo giving up their livelihood for others. In fact, Tolkien, who rankled at any suggestion that his work was complex allegory or symbolism, wrote that the main theme of The Lord of the Rings is about "death and the desire for deathlessness."[172]

Wonderful stories tell us something about death. What about the fading of promises, intellect, and beauty? And what about the death of those I love? The death of a loved one is an earthquake that profoundly destabilizes us, with aftershocks that keep reverberating through our lives. Because our identities and stories are inextricably linked with those whom we love, upon their death we lose ourselves and face trying to rebuild. The most effective storytellers accept death as a central human experience and find ways to be courageous, kind, and even hopeful in light of this reality.

The life worth living relates to dying and facing death. It is difficult to achieve any form of scientific, humanitarian, or artistic greatness without sacrifice. It is hard to raise a healthy child without sacrifice. Warring factions in Northern Ireland or South Africa did not achieve peace without sacrifice. Nelson Mandela titled his 1964 speech at his trial where he was sentenced to life in prison, "I Am Prepared to Die." After twenty-seven years in prison, Mandela continued this way of living by exhibiting forgiveness and reconciliation, modeling the wisdom of Joseph Campbell, "The hero of yesterday becomes the tyrant of tomorrow, unless he crucifies *himself* today."[173]

Think about rights for slaves, for blacks, for women, for African Americans, for LGBTQ people, for children, and environmental protections—these were not handed to us on a silver platter and many came with substantial cost. People fought for them, sacrificed their wellbeing, jobs, careers, relationships, even their lives. Many people have risked their lives or livelihood to expose the truth. They "died" to what others thought of them, "died" to their own comforts, desires for power, pleasure, and wealth. They gave up many personal goals and ambitions and took on the burden of misunderstanding, condemnation, and abandonment. This manner of living is not passivity—a servility to the whims of others. In fact, to challenge injustice takes heroic effort and confronting evil requires sacrifice. Embedded structural evils are not going to give up without a fight and overcoming our entrenched beliefs will require courage. Those with vested interests, money, influence, and power will not give these up today to save the planet for tomorrow. Usually, we want success without failure; we want comfort without suffering, pain, or cost; we want the world transformed without risk or struggle.

When viewed in terms of the past, the concept of sacrifice is violent and torturous. The idea of sacrifice has also been manipulatively used, for example, against women and slaves when urged to "sacrifice" and accept their oppression, or for soldiers urged to sacrifice for a nation waging aggressive war. Alcoholics, drug addicts, and abusers often want other people to sacrifice. And how many codependents have sadly sacrificed their lives and wellbeing for the wrong reasons? But today, sacrifice can be purged of its gore and manipulation, and given a relational redefinition—one that has a noble quality, where we admire those who risk or sacrifice their livelihood or lives for the sake of others.

The idea of sacrifice—death as a way to life—is central to many Christian stories. In addition, essential Christian themes such as repentance, faithfulness, hope, and love can be conceived as sacrifice. To repent is to turn around and die to a wrong way of relating. Faithfulness requires the death of false beliefs. To hope involves dying to the striving for immediate fulfillment. The greatest love, according to the Christian story, is to give up one's life for the sake of others.

For Christianity to transform itself and promote the life worth living, according to its own message, it is going to have to die. This death will include dying to zero-sum games. This death will include repenting for the stories that have caused chaos, misery, death, and intellectual inebriation. This will include giving up its fight with modern science, lest it succumb to ignorance and delusion. This will include dying to all those beliefs and practices that fail a relational test as seen in all the people harmed in the church's history, including slaves, blacks, women, heretics, pagans, Jews, children, LGBTQ people, members of other religions, agnostics, and atheists.

> Death destroys a man: the idea of Death saves him.
> —E. M. Forster[174]

Death gives life a strange duality—a poignant beauty and tragedy, an extraordinary wonder of aliveness and a sense of precarious frailty. Death and the life worth living have an inextricable connection. Death instructs us about life. Because death gives us a time limit, we must decide on what to spend our energy. We all live with limitation. Even the brightest among us can only become expert in one, or possibly two, specialized areas. Even the most altruistic have limited resources to engage social or environmental problems. Knowing our mortality can help filter out superfluous activities, projects, or goals, and help focus on what we want to achieve. More importantly, it focuses us on who we want to be. Death gives an urgency to the life worth living. Death gives us pause—to question our relationships so far, especially how we treat the outsider.[175] *Memento mori*—remember that you must die.

A new being human

Judging from the many dystopian novels and zombie apocalypses, the outlook for the future appears bleak. There are reasons for pessimism. We are facing a sixth mass extinction and environmental catastrophe if we choose not to change our unsupportable ways. We are racing toward a point of no return—water shortages, pollution, melting ice caps and glaciers, species depletion, rain forests falling to logging and farming, and unsustainable consumer capitalism. The poor suffer and the rich fatten themselves, becoming the new lords over a feudal class strapped to their debt. We have government corruption, too much power in the hands of the wealthy, high incarceration rates, and unnecessary and unjust wars.

Ten years after the invasion of Iraq, the figures were of at least 190,000 direct war deaths (most were Iraqi civilians) and a cost of two trillion dollars.[176] Four million people were forced to leave their homes and thousands more were wounded. Back in the United States, a veteran commits suicide once every sixty-five minutes. And the architects of this catastrophe still smugly walk the earth and refuse to recognize their mendacity or the evil of their actions. In the main lobby of the CIA etched into the wall are the words from the Gospel of John, "And ye shall know the truth and the truth shall make you free," providing yet another example of the malleability of Bible verses. Yes, we know the truth of drone strikes, black prisons, assassinations, overthrowing elected leaders in foreign countries, supplying arms, backing wars, torture, and other human rights violations. We know the truth from the CIA report on torture that explicitly states that *yes* we tortured many people, and *no* there was not any useful information that thwarted terrorist attacks (something they could have learned from psychologists years ago).[177] We have become like those we condemn.

What professions have the most psychopaths? Research finds that in the top ten, CEOs are first. Also making the top ten list are, unsurprisingly, lawyers and clergy.[178] Sadly, many humans favor disastrous, psychopathic leadership. Fish rot from the head. Crap rises to the top. Choose your cliché—there are plenty, and for good reason. Dumbledore, in Harry Potter, channeling Plato, noted the depressing fact that the people who should be in power don't want it. And if those at the top are not psychopathic, many are narcissistic. Everything is about them and feeling powerful and heroic. Let's just lay off these workers because it will make us feel important, decisive, and get us more money. Or let's just bomb another country, not because any studies show it will make the situation better, but because it will make us look brave, righteous, and heroic. We did the "right" thing—too bad for the poor suckers on the receiving end.

Of course, we could go on, but airing grievances is only part of a solution. The great musician and activist Pete Seeger said, "The key to the future of the world is finding the optimistic stories and letting them be known."[179] Optimistic stories differ from happy stories. Tolstoy in his famous opening line of Anna Karenina wrote, "All happy families are alike, each unhappy family is unhappy in its own way."[180] There is nothing interesting or exciting about an entirely cheerful story. Complete happiness is bland. What would a novel be like if it was all about one happy family? Perfect bliss is boring. Dante's *Inferno* is popular, but few mortals have read all of *Paradise*. C. S. Lewis, who wrote *The Screwtape Letters*, containing letters from a senior devil Screwtape to a young apprentice Wormwood, noted that the devilish advice ought to have been balanced with a book on advice from an archangel. Lewis confessed, however, that he lacked the ability to imagine how this perfect archangel would talk and relate.[181] No wonder. Perfection is flat and flavorless. Would an angel even have a sense of humor? How could an archangel beat Screwtape's opening in his last letter: "My dear, my very dear, Wormwood, my poppet, my pigsnie"?[182]

Steven Pinker's *The Better Angels of Our Nature*, to which we have referred, is an optimistic story. The book is not a cheerful story, with its catalogue of violence across the centuries. It is, however, optimistic. Violence has declined. We are better off than we were in the past, but this doesn't mean that societies will necessarily stay this way, and it doesn't mean that we don't face considerable problems. Pinker and others have noted significant ethical advancements since the Second World War: the advancement of rights for blacks, African Americans, women, gays, children, and animals. We have apartheid declared a crime against humanity, and rape during war declared a war crime. We have the decline of corporal punishment (with psychologists now agreeing that parents should never spank children), the increasing awareness of cruelty to animals, and wider concern for our impact on our climate and environment. Even wars conducted today are in marked contrast to the thousand-bomber raids and nuclear weapons use of World War II. There is reason for hope.

To promote a life worth living, we need optimistic stories that show that if humanity is undermined anywhere, it is undermined everywhere. This is the spirit of the word *Ubuntu*. The word gained prominence in post-apartheid South Africa and speaks of living in community with generosity toward others. As Tutu puts it, *Ubuntu* means, "My humanity is caught up, is inextricably bound up, in yours," so that we can only be humans together.[183] In this regard, the most important battle is between those who are for widening relationships and those who are not—between those who are constructive and those who are destructive. Whether you are a Christian, secular humanist, or member of another religion, are you for stories and strategies that can join us all together rather than rip us apart? Group myths once helped us in the past to survive, but now they are instigators of exclusion, hubris, and violence. We need reconfigured or new stories that no longer work just for our coalition, but are planetary—including all humanity and other creatures and life forms with whom we share the planet.

Against these ideas is sometimes the howling objection: By forcing me to include others, you are excluding me! This would be a funny comment if it wasn't true. When Pope Francis urged the wealthy to give more to the poor, Ken Langone, a Catholic and billionaire founder of Home Depot, moaned about the pope's "exclusionary" remarks.[184] We hear a similar response in the gay rights discussion. "What—you want to allow gays to marry? That is excluding my [exclusive] views." My views don't allow for including these folks, whoever they may be—gays, women, blacks, Muslims, Jews, Iranians, or other riffraff. The Sultan of Brunei recently imposed the sanction of "death by stoning" for gay sex. Following the international outcry, Brunei wrote to the European Union calling for "tolerance, respect, and understanding" regarding the country's position on traditional values.[185]

Game theory answers these objections. Those holding these exclusive views are defectors trying to game the system for their advantage. Those who play finite, zero-sum games—where a win for them is a loss for others—are threatened by positive sum and infinite games, which they rightly understand to be devastating to their games. Telling narratives that include all humanity is not, however, an exclusion, but a retaliation for a defection, a rebuke, or a strong invitation to stop playing zero-sum games. It is a refusal to play zero-sum games or play finite games as if they matter. It is an invitation into a different, viable game where rules of exclusion are not part of the game. In summary, in terms of game theory, let us be clear (have clarity of intentions), cooperative, and trustworthy (including with outsiders), forgive others, repent of failures, and stand up to injustice (rebuke defectors).

On the question of gay rights, we would be remiss not to address the debate involving one of the most vilified groups in the world today, the LGBTQ community. Large swaths of Christianity oppose gay relationships, from Eastern Orthodox to Roman Catholic to Protestant. The Russian Orthodox Church has given support to the criminalization of gay relationships. Cardinal Raymond Burke, once second to Pope Francis, called for parents to shield their kids from gay relatives (Cardinal Burke was thankfully removed). Even the more progressive Pope Francis still supports the church's teaching that homosexual acts are sin. Evangelicals have largely given up fighting over women in ministry. Now their war is over gays.

Drawing from the material already covered, we can provide summary answers for why most of Christianity has gone horribly wrong regarding the treatment of LGBTQ people and that there are resources within Christianity for transformation.

First, if churches have been wrong about creation, women, slavery, apartheid, birth control, corporal punishment, and other things, it shows that more self-criticism is required. Instead of providing moral clarity on human rights for slaves and women, many churches went in precisely the wrong direction. At the very least, it opens the possibility that they may be wrong on gay rights.

Second, it should be obvious by now that Christians will not find any consensus on this issue by an appeal to the Bible. We have covered many diverse stories, all derived from the Bible. Opposing positions are created by selectively elevating some passages or themes over others. Even the same passage can yield opposite positions. Is the story of Sodom and Gomorrah a story that condemns homosexuality, or a lack of hospitality and injustice? Some interpreters look to Ezekiel 16:49, "This was the guilt of your sister Sodom: she and her daughters had pride, excess of food, and prosperous ease, but did not aid the poor and needy." Does Paul in Romans 1 condemn homosexuality as we understand it today, especially considering that the ancient world had no word or concept for "homosexuality"? Others, however, argue that Paul in 1 Corinthians 6:9 unambiguously opposed homosexuality. Like a multitude of other debates, the Bible is read in diverse ways. For instance, Richard Hayes, professor of New Testament at Duke University, in his well-regarded *The Moral Vision of the New Testament*, acknowledges the antisemitism in the New Testament, but argues that the New Testament's position on homosexuality is that it is unequivocally a sin.[186] Whereas Dale

Martin, professor of Religious Studies at Yale University, in *Sex and the Single Savior*, finds other ways to read the New Testament. He argues that one way to read the stories of Jesus is through the "gay imagination," as nowhere is Jesus said to have loved a woman. There was, however, the disciple that Jesus loved (John 13:23–25), that Jesus looked at the rich young ruler and loved him (Mark 10:21), that when Jesus weeps at Lazarus' tomb, people said "see how he loved him" (John 11:36), and Jesus, according to Martin, "flirts" with Peter and asks him three times, "Do you *really* love me?" (John 21:15–19).[187] Similar to the debates over slavery, apartheid, and women, the debate over gays won't find resolution by an appeal to the Bible. The outcome depends on what Christians emphasize, which leads to a third point.

Third, the LGBTQ community qualifies as one of the most excluded and vilified communities today. Therefore, the stories of Jesus with the excluded—with tax collectors, Samaritans, the poor, widows, and other rejected people—should be brought to the forefront of religious imagination and practice. Central themes in the gospel story, such as love, freedom, and all people made in the image of God, come into play. The Apostle Paul's arguments for including gentiles, his promotion of women in ministry, and his commands to masters and slaves (which if consistently applied would abolish slavery), are further examples to illustrate a new positive-sum-game that includes LGBTQ people. Christianity could be reconfigured as an infinite game, where no one loses, including LGBTQ people.

Fourth, there is the irreparable harm done to gay people, and most grievously to gay children. This enormous body of evidence clearly fails the relational test. Here are three examples:

The first of Ryan Kendall, who testified in the Hollingsworth vs. Perry case, the landmark 2010 Supreme Court case that overturned California's Proposition 8, which had banned gay marriage. Ryan testified to undergoing forced conversion therapy as a teenager that almost drove him to suicide. He also stated on the stand that his mother, an evangelical Christian, had told him she would've rather had an abortion than had a gay son.

The second of Ryan Robertson who, when he was twelve years old, came out to his parents as gay. His parents, who were faithful Christians, urged him to hate and fight against these sexual desires and to follow Jesus. Ryan met weekly with his pastor and attended reparative therapy. By eighteen years old, however, he had had enough, ran away from home, and became addicted to drugs. Ryan died of a heroin overdose, only twenty years old. His parents, Rob and Linda Robertson, later changed their views and are now active in speaking for the gay community.

The third of the wonderful and brilliant neurologist Oliver Sacks, who recounts what happened when his mother found out he was gay:

"When I was twenty-one and home from college, I accompanied my father one evening on his rounds. We were driving in the car, and he asked me how things were going. Fine. Did I have any girlfriends? No. Why didn't I have any girlfriends? I guessed I didn't like girls... Silence for a few moments... Does that mean you like boys? Yes, I replied, I am a homosexual.

"I asked my father not to mention this to my mother under any circumstances: it would break her heart—she'd never understand. The next morning, my mother came tearing down the stairs, shrieking at me, hurling Deuteronomical curses, horrible judgmental accusations. This went on for an hour. Then she fell silent. She remained completely silent for three days, after which normalcy returned. The subject was never mentioned again during her lifetime."[188]

Thankfully, many of those Christian groups in the "gay cure" therapy movement have shut down. Exodus International, which for thirty-seven years sought to change people's sexual orientation, closed its doors with its founder Alan Chambers (who came out as gay) issuing an apology to the LGBTQ community and admitting that of the people he met, 99 percent haven't changed their sexual orientation. Or as another example, McKrae Game, the founder of one of the largest conversion therapy organizations, also apologized for his behavior and came out as gay.[189] Some Christians still argue that gays can change from their "sinful lifestyle" and "pray away the gay"; however, any evidence for this change of sexual orientation is microscopic to nonexistent.

The intense opposition to homosexuality surely has multiple causes. For one, there is the well-known observation by psychologists of people moralizing their own distaste for something. This occurs along the lines of "I have no attraction for the same sex; therefore same-sex relationships must be immoral." For another, there are studies showing that those with the greatest hostility toward gays may have same-sex attraction.[190] I have lost count of how many people who were once virulently anti-homosexual, but who later came out as gay.

Fifth, and finally, if sin is defined as "relational failure," what then is wrong with two consenting adults living together and being in love? With sin defined relationally, homosexuals aren't sinners. The twist in the tale is that the sinners are those who vilify, exclude, and condemn gays. Once again, following the stories about Jesus in the Gospels—the religious experts are wrong and misapply the label "sinner." Relationships transform. We don't need a Gallup poll to show that people who know a gay person are much more inclined to approve of gay marriage.[191] As people relate with gays, they discover gays are people just like them, not the evil caricature that their group assigned to them. Bigots intuitively know this relational fact by claiming the old diversionary trope "I have gay friends," or "Some of my best friends are Jews," or "I have a good black friend from school." They also intuitively know that relationships transform, hence part of the reason they isolate their group. In a final desperate move, they sometimes claim, "You say that homosexuals just want to be treated like everyone else. What's next—pedophilia or marrying your pet goat?" Such statements simply reveal an utterly morally bankrupt way of thinking that cannot distinguish between two consenting adults, and the abuse of power, exploitation of younger people, or torturing weaker species—animals that are unable to give consent.

* * *

I remarked in the introduction that Christianity has an ambiguous and troubled relationship with the good life. Great Christian reformers are too often the exception rather than the rule. Even today, Christianity is once again lagging by actively opposing full human rights for the LBGTQ community. Even so, Christianity boldly promises to aid the life worth living. Christianity, however, has resources within itself for its own transformation—including considering disruptive influences, examining itself through the light of others, recognizing its own relational failures, repentance, testing all outcomes relationally, living faithfully with others, addressing the insider-outsider divide, dying for the sake of others, and telling fruitful stories and rejecting the rotten.

The quest for the life worth living has surely led many to leave Christianity—for reasons we have already covered, such as the central importance of relationships, love, truth, living in light of reality as we understand it today, a desire for positive-sum games, and a desire for relationships with outsiders that are on an equal footing. For those remaining within Christianity, significant challenges remain. There is the ongoing challenge to keep one's stories meshed with reality and modern science. There is the challenge to transform these stories and for these stories to remain "good news" for people in the twenty-first century. There is the challenge of confronting and rebuking all those who proliferate toxic or downright dangerous Christian stories. There is the challenge to overcome the insider-outsider divide and the tendency that any religion has toward protecting ingroups.

For those outside Christianity, there are ways to enjoy and benefit from some Christian stories—whether portrayed in writing, art, or music.

These stories and metaphors can aid in the quest for the life worth living. In fact, we could argue that these stories are best viewed from an outside, secular point of view. When humanity made the jump to postulate supernatural entities, it traveled on a road away from reality. By engaging in imaginary battles and conversations with a supernatural world, it cemented a mistaken view of the world, elevated magical thinking, and erected barriers with outsiders. A modern secular humanist can still find value in Christian stories and metaphors. They can select whatever stories they enjoy—without the constraints that belief in these stories place on current knowledge, relationships, and ethics.

We need optimistic stories, positive-sum games, infinite games where games continue with no winner. This is not a requirement to play nice all the time—like my Maine Coon cat who is usually sweet but will bite when provoked. There are still plenty of people with their zero-sum games, rules of exclusion, jostling for power, and who cry "exclusion" when challenged. The answer is not to give in and lose. Living optimistic stories and playing infinite games will require a stand against psychopaths, narcissists, hateful or greedy groups, exploiters of others or the environment, aggressive nations, and people who deny human rights. We need compassion, but compassion is vulnerable. Hackers and swindlers notoriously exploit compassion to gain entry into secure systems or people's wallets. We need trust, but some take advantage of trusting individuals. In the end, we also need a healthy dose of skepticism and a willingness to retaliate when necessary.

Faced with sometimes considerable opposition, can our tiny contribution matter? Call it the butterfly effect or the snowball effect. Insignificant things can add up over time. In our interconnected world, the small act of kindness can cascade into an avalanche of change. One brief act of opposing an injustice can amplify through the entire system.

A new way of being human is opening and expanding our relationships in positive, constructive, and optimistic ways. Life in this new world follows the analogy of a cell—it has boundaries of a cellular wall that contain its specific identity, but it is permeable. Osmosis allows nutrients to flow in and out. Its life and vitality depend on it. So does ours.

Endnotes

1. As recounted to us by Plato in his *Apology*, 38a. Socrates gave this statement after his conviction for disrespecting the gods and corrupting the youth of Athens.
2. In Greek mythology, King Sisyphus was punished for his misdeeds—eternally consigned to absurd and futile hard labor—by being made to endlessly roll a boulder up a hill, only to have it roll back down again, just before he reached the top.
3. Carreyrou, *Bad Blood*.
4. Tarico, "Surprise! Atheist Marriages May Last Longer Than Christian Ones."
5. Freud, *Future of an Illusion*, 56–57.
6. Pinker, *Better Angels of Our Nature*, 676–78.
7. Pinker, *Better Angels of Our Nature*, 475.
8. For an overview, see Bellamy, "Manoeuvre Warfare," 541–44.
9. Sun Tzu, *Art of War*, 16.
10. The French also added additional weaker fortifications to complete the line to the English Channel.
11. Lewin, *Rommel as Military Commander*, 221.
12. Leonhard, *Art of Maneuver*, 61–76.
13. The angel in a wrestling match with Jacob dislocates Jacob's hip, rendering his strength irrelevant and beginning the transformation of Jacob's life (Gen 32:25).
14. Leonhard, *Art of Maneuver*, 79–80.
15. Shepard, *Moon Shot*, chapter 24.
16. Cousins, "Rendezvous with Infinity."
17. Conrad, *Lord Jim*, 73.
18. Lee, To Kill a Mockingbird, 174.
19. Fine, *Mind of Its Own*, 108–09.
20. Fine, *Mind of Its Own*, 89.
21. Fine, *Mind of Its Own*, 106.

22. Uys, The Gods Must Be Crazy.
23. Lake Wobegon is Garrison Keillor's fictional town in Minnesota, where, it is said, "all the women are strong, all the men are good-looking, and all the children are above average."
24. Rodrigues, "George Carlin - Idiot and Maniac."
25. Wikipedia, "List of Cognitive Biases."
26. Feldman, *Liar in Your Life*, 31, 38.
27. Today, most consider the use of weapons of mass destruction against civilians to be a war crime. A separate issue is whether the use of atomic weapons shortened the war. The war was at an end. Japan was surrounded, its resources depleted, its navy and air force destroyed. Japan was losing cities from conventional bombs and the Soviets had entered the war. In addition, several top US generals and admirals, such as Eisenhower, Nimitz, Leahy, and MacArthur, opposed dropping atomic weapons.
28. Arbesman, *Half-Life of Facts*.
29. Arbesman, *Half-Life of Facts*, chapter 3, section 2.
30. Quoidbach, Gilbert, and Wilson, "The End of History Illusion."
31. The Prophet Nathan's approach to King David, who ensnared the king through clever storytelling (2 Sam 12:1–15).
32. Feynman, *Surely You're Joking*, 343.
33. Bierce, *Devil's Dictionary*, 113.
34. de Sales, *Introduction to the Devout Life*, 196.
35. Marshall, *Chicago*.
36. Chabris and Simons, "Invisible Gorilla."
37. Wikipedia, "*Search for Signs of Intelligent Life*."
38. Wachowski and Wachowski, Matrix.
39. Plato, *Apology*, 38a.
40. Solzhenitsyn, *Gulag Archipelago*, 75.
41. The most famous experiments were done by Yale psychologist Stanley Milgram. Ordinary people will follow orders from an authority figure and inflict pain on others. Given power, some will become sadists.
42. Sartre, *No Exit*.
43. Fitzgerald, *Great Gatsby*, 4.
44. Berra, *The Yogi Book*, "I didn't really say everything I said."
45. Captain Francesco Schettino was later sentenced to sixteen years in jail for manslaughter. Kingston, "Captain who commanded Costa Concordia in cruise disaster."
46. Cleese and Booth, *Fawlty Towers*, "The Wedding Party."
47. Tavris and Aronson, *Mistakes Were Made*, 2.
48. Tavris and Aronson, *Mistakes Were Made*, 1.
49. Tavris and Aronson, *Mistakes Were Made*, 2.

50. Tavris and Aronson, *Mistakes Were Made*, 9.
51. Malkin and Stein, *Eichmann in My Hands*.
52. Arendt, *Eichmann in Jerusalem*.
53. Tavris and Aronson, *Mistakes Were Made*, 9–10.
54. Smith, "Sorry, But Not Sorry."
55. Anderson, *Sin: A History*, 16.
56. A concept present in Christian and Jewish reflection and implicit in many places in the Hebrew Bible and New Testament.
57. Goleman, *Social Intelligence*.
58. Lieberman, *Social*.
59. See Shults, *Christology and Science*, 24–28.
60. LeRon Shults's phrase. See, for example, his discussion on the philosophical turn to relationality in Shults, *Reforming the Doctrine of God*, 5–9.
61. Hoffman, *The Man Who Loved Only Numbers*.
62. A relational emphasis also lends itself to redefining other things relationally as well, for example, masculinity. No matter how we characterize masculinity, it should be done relationally; that is, to connect it with women and reject any idea or manifestation of masculinity that subordinates, demeans, or harms women.
63. Hugo, *Les Misérables*, Part I, Book 8, Section IV.
64. Taibbi, "Cruel and Unusual Punishment."
65. Asimov, *Foundation*, 143.
66. Levi, *If This Is a Man*, 35.
67. Yancey, *What's So Amazing about Grace?*, 54.
68. Wright, *Going Clear*, 248–49.
69. Bonhoeffer, *Cost of Discipleship*, 44–45.
70. Williams, *Tokens of Trust*, 152.
71. Rowling, *Deathly Hallows*, 103.
72. Rowling, *Deathly Hallows*, 741.
73. Ivanhoe, *Daodejing of Laozi*, 33.
74. Pinker, *Better Angels of Our Nature*, 506.
75. Eve LaPlante, a direct descendant of Sewall, wrote an intriguing and moving account of his life in her book: LaPlante, *Salem Witch Judge*. The details on Sewell that follow are taken from her material.
76. LaPlante, *Salem Witch Judge*, 300–304.
77. LaPlante, *Salem Witch Judge*, 304–11. The full title was "Talitha Cumi: Or an Invitation to Women to Look after Their Inheritance in the Heavenly Mansions." *Talitha Cumi* refers to the Aramaic in Mark 5:41: "Little girl, stand up." Sewell probably wrote this at the deathbed of his daughter.

78. Tutu, *No Future without Forgiveness*.

79. Tutu, *No Future without Forgiveness*, chapter 2.

80. A silver talent was worth approximately six thousand denarii, and one denarius was the standard daily wage. Just one silver talent was worth about sixteen years of wages, so ten thousand talents is a high credit balance.

81. Lomax, *Railway Man*, 123–24.

82. Lomax, *Railway Man*, 116.

83. Lomax, *Railway Man*, 262–63.

84. Lomax, *Railway Man*, 274.

85. Lomax, *Railway Man*, 275.

86. Khazan, "The Forgiveness Boost."

87. Axelrod, *Evolution of Cooperation*, 3.

88. Radiolab podcast found here: https://www.wnycstudios.org/podcasts/radiolab/segments/104010-one-good-deed-deserves-another.

89. Carse, *Finite and Infinite Games*, 3.

90. Carse, *Finite and Infinite Games*, 83.

91. Pinker, *Better Angels of our Nature*, 586–90.

92. Carroll, "Great Time for Reason and Science."

93. The following two examples are adapted from: Williams, *Maleness of Jesus*, 98–103, 106–07.

94. Repcheck, *Man Who Found Time*.

95. Repcheck, *Man Who Found Time*, 152–53.

96. Repcheck, *Man Who Found Time*, 1.

97. Carroll, *Endless Forms Most Beautiful*, 9.

98. Carroll, *Endless Forms Most Beautiful*, 139, 145.

99. Tyson, "The good thing."

100. Greene, *Hidden Reality*, 3–11.

101. Wikipedia, "All models are wrong."

102. Siegel, "Dark Energy."

103. Prothero, *Evolution*, 54–58.

104. Finkelstein and Silberman, *Bible Unearthed*.

105. Ehrman, *Misquoting Jesus*, 8–9.

106. From William of Occam, a fourteenth century theologian and philosopher, who stated, "Entities should not be multiplied unnecessarily." Among competing explanations or theories, the simpler one is better.

107. Allison, *New Moses*.

108. See, for example, Allison, *New Moses*, 195.

109. Likewise with Matthew's account of the death of Jesus: the sun went dark, the temple veil was torn in two, an earthquake occurred, and then a small zombie apocalypse occurred with those who rose from their graves and entered Jerusalem (Matt 27:45–54). None of these events are recorded by anyone else.

110. Schweitzer, *Quest of the Historical Jesus*, 398–403.

111. Crossan, *Historical Jesus*, xxviii.

112. Ehrman, *Did Jesus Exist?* 42–45.

113. Bruce, *New Testament Documents*, 119.

114. For a comprehensive defense of the mythic position, see Carrier, *On the Historicity of Jesus*.

115. Williams, *Maleness of Jesus*.

116. Carl Sagan's evocative phrase and title of his book: *The Demon-Haunted World: Science as a Candle in the Dark*.

117. See Girard, *Violence and the Sacred*. Also Girard, *Scapegoat*.

118. Jenson, *Systematic Theology*, 186.

119. Philippe, *People vs. George Lucas*.

120. Taylor, *How Star Wars Conquered the Universe*, 57.

121. Taylor, *How Star Wars Conquered the Universe*, 62.

122. Press Association, "J. K. Rowling: Hermione Should Have Married Harry, Not Ron."

123. Monteiro, "Emma Watson UN Speech."

124. Keller, *Reason for God*, 52.

125. Keller, *Reason for God*, 52–53.

126. Keller *Reason for God*, 56.

127. Keller, *Reason for God*, 57.

128. Keller *Reason for God*, 53.

129. Keller *Reason for God*, 54.

130. Keller, *Reason for God*, 63–67.

131. Erickson, *Complicity in the Holocaust*, 8.

132. Erickson, *Complicity in the Holocaust*, 37. See also Solberg, *A Church Undone*.

133. Erickson, *Complicity in the Holocaust*, 127.

134. Erickson, *Complicity in the Holocaust*, 25.

135. Douglass, *Narrative*, 55.

136. Douglass, *Narrative*, 72.

137. Haley, "Martin Luther King Jr.: Playboy Interview (1965)."

138. Tomcat, "Atheists for Jesus."

139. Flew, *Thinking Straight*, 47.

140. Pinker, *Better Angels of Our Nature*, 6.

141. God's plan and decision from eternity that some will be saved and granted eternal life, and others (the wicked) consigned to eternal torment.

142. Calvin, *Institutes* 3.23.7.

143. Lewis, *Problem of Pain*, 118.

144. Pro-slavery advocate John Hopkins said, "If it were a matter to be determined by my personal sympathies, tastes, or feelings, I should be as ready as any man to condemn the institution of slavery; for all my prejudices of education, habit, and social position stand entirely opposed to it." Hopkins, *Scriptural, Ecclesiastical, and Historical View of Slavery*, 6.

145. For example, conservative New Testament scholar Thomas Schreiner said to a friend who held an egalitarian view of 1 Timothy 2:9–15, "I would like to believe the position you hold. But it seems as if you have to leap over the evidence of the text to espouse such a position." In Schreiner, "An Interpretation of 1 Timothy 2:9–15," 106.

146. DebatesOnline, "Richard Dawkins, Christopher Hitchens, Sam Harris, Daniel Dennett."

147. Flood, "Bible Becomes 2011 Bestseller in Norway."

148. We may call this relational test an "insider test for faith," in contrast to John Loftus's "outsider test for faith," where he urges Christians to examine their own faith with the same level of skepticism and critical analysis as they would with any other religion. See Loftus, *Outsider Test for Faith*.

149. For example, the Christian pro-slavery movement reinterpreted the Golden Rule as "I should treat my slaves the way I would like to be treated if I was a slave." Of course, that didn't mean setting slaves free. The rule wasn't to treat slaves how *they* would like to be treated. Pro-slavery ideology incorporated love into its system so that its champions even viewed the Golden Rule to support slavery. Southern theologian James H. Thornwell wrote, "The rule then simply requires, in the case of Slavery, that we should treat our slaves as we should feel that we had a right to be treated if we were slaves ourselves." Thornwell, *Collected Writings*, 429.

150. The famous and violent abolitionist John Brown, however, took a fancy to switching this around. He emphasized that God had drowned Pharaoh's army, and his favorite texts were an "eye for an eye" and "without the shedding of blood there is no remission of sin." McPherson, *Battle Cry of Freedom*, 84, 152, 203.

151. Craig, "#16 Slaughter of the Canaanites."

152. Wright, *Going Clear*.

153. For example, Winston, "Leading Atheist, Accused of Sexual Misconduct, Speaks Out."

154. Darley and Batson, "From Jerusalem to Jericho."

155. Bierce, *Devil's Dictionary*, 34.

156. Says the Queen to Alice in Carroll, *Through the Looking Glass*, 103.

ENDNOTES

157. Girard, *Red Violin*.
158. See Fritz et al., "Player Preferences." Also, Barclay, "Stradivarius Pseudoscience." Or this anecdote by a musician who didn't realize he was playing a Stradivarius violin: Brooks, "My Stradivarius Moment."
159. Campbell, *The Power of Myth*, 206.
160. Barna Group, "Six Reasons Young Christians Leave Church."
161. Harris, *End of Faith*, 106.
162. Shults, "Theology after Pandora," 363.
163. Shults, *Practicing Safe Sects*, 166–67.
164. Lewis-Williams, *Conceiving God*, 143.
165. Shults, "Science and Religious Supremacy," 86.
166. Shults draws attention to these difficulties in, for example, Shults, *Theology after the Birth of God*, 99–102.
167. McLaughlin, *The Neurotic's Notebook*, 72.
168. For example, Shults, *Theology after the Birth of God*, 56.
169. Noll, *The Civil War as a Theological Crisis*, 50.
170. As noted by Shults, *Iconoclastic Theology*, 2.
171. Greig, "There Would Be So Much to Tell Her."
172. J. R. R. Tolkien, *Letters*, no. 203.
173. Campbell, *Hero with a Thousand Faces*, 353.
174. Foster, Howards End, 273.
175. And when considering "dying" or "death" we need to focus self-consciously on *outsiders*, because studies in mortality salience or "terror management theory" (when we think about our own inevitable death) have shown the tendency to increase in-group thinking and protection. In other words, when considering the topic of death, we have the tendency to become insular, protective, and more aggressive toward outsiders.
176. Brown University, "Iraq War."
177. See, for example, a summary of seven key points from the torture report: Ashkenas et al., "7 Key Points from the CIA Torture Report."

    And there is much we still don't know. See Ladin, "There's So Much We Still Don't Know."
178. Dutton, *Wisdom of Psychopaths*, 161–62.
179. Quoted in Pareles, "Pete Seeger."
180. Tolstoy, Anna Karenina, 3.
181. Lewis, *Screwtape Letters*, xiv.
182. Lewis, *Screwtape Letters*, 145.
183. Tutu, *No Future without Forgiveness*, 31.

184. Reported by CNBC: Caruso-Cabrera, "Pope's Sharp Words Make a Wealthy Donor Hesitate."
185. Boffey, "Brunei Defends Death by Stoning."
186. Hayes, *Moral Vision of the New Testament*, 389, 394, 400, 403.
187. Martin, *Sex and the Single Savior*, 99–100.
188. Quoted in Weschler, "A Rare, Personal Look."
189. Iati, "Conversion Therapy Center Founder."
190. Bryner, "Study: Homophobes May Be Hidden Homosexuals."
191. Morales, "Knowing Someone Gay/ Lesbian Affects Views of Gay Issues."

Bibliography

Allison, Dale C., Jr. *The New Moses: A Matthean Typology*. Minneapolis: Fortress, 1993.
Anderson, Gary. *Sin: A History*. New Haven, CT: Yale University Press, 2009.
Arbesman, Samuel. *The Half-Life of Facts: Why Everything We Know Has an Expiration Date*. New York: Current, 2012.
Arendt, Hannah. *Eichmann in Jerusalem: A Report on the Banality of Evil*. New York: Penguin, 2006.
Ashkenas, Jeremy, et al. "7 Key Points from the CIA Torture Report." *The New York Times*, December 9, 2014.
Asimov, Isaac. *Foundation*. New York: Bantam Books, 2004.
Axelrod, Robert. *The Evolution of Cooperation*. Rev. ed. New York: Basic Books, 2006.
Barclay, R. L. "Stradivarius Pseudoscience: The Myth of the Miraculous Musical Instrument." *Skeptic Magazine* 16.2 (2011) 45–50.
Barna Group. "Six Reasons Young Christians Leave Church." https://www.barna.com/research/six-reasons-young-christians-leave-church/.
Bellamy, Christopher. "Manoeuvre Warfare." In *The Oxford Companion to Military History*, edited by Richard Holmes, 541–44. Oxford: Oxford University Press, 2001.
Berra, Yogi. *The Yogi Book*. New York: Workman, 1998.
Bierce, Ambrose. *The Devil's Dictionary*. Mineola, NY: Dover, 1993.
Boffey, Daniel. "Brunei Defends Death by Stoning for Gay Sex in Letter to EU." *The Guardian* April 22, 2019. https://www.theguardian.com/world/2019/apr/22/brunei-defends-stoning-death-gay-sex-letter-eu.
Bonhoeffer, Dietrich. *The Cost of Discipleship*. New York: Touchstone, 1995.
Brooks, Richard. "My Stradivarius Moment." *Violinist.com* April 16, 2020. https://www.violinist.com/blog/rbelecviolinist2138/20204/28202/.
Brown University. "Iraq War: 190,000 lives, $2.2 Trillion." *Costs of War Project* March 14, 2013. http://news.brown.edu/articles/2013/03/warcosts.
Bryner, Jeanna. "Study: Homophobes May Be Hidden Homosexuals." *LiveScience* April 9, 2012. https://www.livescience.com/19563-homophobia-hidden-homosexuals.html.
Bruce, F. F. *The New Testament Documents: Are They Reliable?* 5th rev. ed. Grand Rapids: Eerdmans, 1994.
Calvin, John. *Institutes of the Christian Religion*. Translated by Henry Beveridge. Edinburgh: The Calvin Translation Society, 1845.

Campbell, Joseph. *The Hero with a Thousand Faces*. 2nd ed. Princeton: Princeton University Press, 1968.

———. *The Power of Myth*. New York: Anchor, 1991.

Carreyrou, John. *Bad Blood: Secrets and Lies in a Silicon Valley Startup*. New York: Alfred A. Knopf, 2018.

Carrier, Richard. *On the Historicity of Jesus: Why We Might Have Reason for Doubt*. Sheffield, UK: Sheffield Phoenix, 2014.

Carroll, Lewis. *Through the Looking Glass*. Philadelphia: Henry Altemus, 1897.

Carroll, Sean B. *Endless Forms Most Beautiful: The New Science of Evo Devo and the Making of the Animal Kingdom*. New York: Norton, 2005.

Carroll, Sean. "A Great Time for Reason and Science." http://www.preposterousuniverse.com/blog/2014/03/19/a-great-time-for-reason-and-science/.

Carse, James. *Finite and Infinite Games: A Vision of Life as Play and Possibility*. New York: Free Press, 1986.

Caruso-Cabrera, Michelle. "Pope's Sharp Words Make a Wealthy Donor Hesitate." *CNBC* December 30, 2019. https://www.cnbc.com/2013/12/30/pope-francis-wealthy-catholic-donors-upset-at-popes-rhetoric-about-rich.html.

Chabris, Christopher, and Daniel Simons. "The Invisible Gorilla." http://www.theinvisiblegorilla.com/gorilla_experiment.html.

Cleese, John, and Connie Booth. Fawlty Towers. Season 1, episode 3, "The Wedding Party." Aired October 3, 1975, on BBC.

Conrad, Joseph. *Lord Jim*. New York: McClure, Phillips, & Co., 1905.

Cousins, Norman. "Rendezvous with Infinity." *Cosmic Search* 1.1 (January 1979). http://www.bigear.org/CSMO/HTML/CS01/cs01p30.htm.

Craig, William Lane. "#16 Slaughter of the Canaanites." *Reasonable Faith* August 6, 2007. https://www.reasonablefaith.org/writings/question-answer/slaughter-of-the-canaanites.

Crossan, John Dominic. *The Historical Jesus: The Life of a Mediterranean Jewish Peasant*. New York: Harper, 1991.

Darley, John M., and C. Daniel Batson. "'From Jerusalem to Jericho': A Study of Situational and Dispositional Variables in Helping Behavior." *Journal of Personality and Social Psychology* 27.1 (1973) 100–108. https://greatergood.berkeley.edu/images/uploads/Darley-JersualemJericho.pdf.

DebatesOnline. "Richard Dawkins, Christopher Hitchens, Sam Harris, Daniel Dennett." *YouTube*. https://www.youtube.com/watch?v=Ha78dcwmERw.

de Sales, Francis. *Introduction to the Devout Life*. Translated and edited by John K. Ryan. New York: Doubleday, 1972.

Douglass, Frederick. *The Narrative of the Life of Frederick Douglass*. Oxford: Oxford University Press, 1999.

Dutton, Kevin. *The Wisdom of Psychopaths: What Saints, Spies, and Serial Killers can Teach Us about Success*. New York: Farrar, Straus, & Giroux, 2012.

Ehrman, Bart D. *Did Jesus Exist? The Historical Argument for Jesus of Nazareth*. New York: HarperOne, 2012.

———. *Misquoting Jesus: The Story Behind Who Changed the Bible and Why*. New York: Harper, 2005.

Erickson, Robert. *Complicity in the Holocaust: Churches and Universities in Nazi Germany*. New York: Cambridge University Press, 2012.

Feldman, Robert. *The Liar in Your Life: The Way to Truthful Relationships*. New York: Twelve Books, 2009.
Feynman, Richard P. *Surely You're Joking, Mr. Feynman!* New York: W. W. Norton, 1997.
Fine, Cordelia. *A Mind of Its Own: How Your Brain Distorts and Deceives*. New York: W. W. Norton, 2006.
Finkelstein, Israel, and Neil Asher Silberman. *The Bible Unearthed: Archeology's New Vision of Ancient Israel and the Origin of Its Sacred Texts*. New York: Touchstone, 2002.
Fitzgerald, F. Scott. *The Great Gatsby*. Varna, Bulgaria: Pretorian Books, 2021.
Flew, Antony. *Thinking Straight*. Buffalo, NY: Prometheus, 1977.
Flood, Alison. "Bible Becomes 2011 Bestseller in Norway." *The Guardian* January 3, 2012. http://www.theguardian.com/books/2012/jan/03/bible-2011-bestseller-norway.
Freud, Sigmund. *The Future of an Illusion*. Translated by W. D. Robson-Scott. New York: Liveright, 1955.
Fritz, Claudia, et al. "Player Preferences among New and Old Violins." *Proceedings of the National Academy of Sciences of the United States of America* 109.3 (2012) 760–63.
Girard, Francois, dir. *The Red Violin*. Burbank, CA: New Line Cinema, 1998.
Girard, René. *The Scapegoat*. Translated by Yvonne Freccero. Baltimore: The John Hopkins University Press, 1986.
———. *Violence and the Sacred*. Translated by Patrick Gregory. Baltimore: The John Hopkins University Press, 1977.
Goleman, Daniel. *Social Intelligence: The New Science of Human Relationships*. New York: Bantam Books, 2006.
Greene, Brian. *The Hidden Reality: Parallel Universes and the Deep Laws of the Cosmos*. New York: Knopf, 2011.
Greig, Geordie. "There Would Be So Much to Tell Her." *The Telegraph* January 10, 2006. https://www.telegraph.co.uk/news/uknews/1507438/There-would-be-so-much-to-tell-her....html.
Haley, Alex. "Martin Luther King Jr.: Playboy Interview (1965)." *Scraps from the Loft* January 1, 2018. https://scrapsfromtheloft.com/politics/martin-luther-king-jr-playboy-interview-1965/.
Harris, Sam. *The End of Faith: Religion, Terror, and the Future of Reason*. New York: W. W. Norton, 2004.
Hayes, Richard B. *The Moral Vision of the New Testament: Community, Cross, New Creation: A Contemporary Introduction to New Testament Ethics*. New York: Harper, 1996.
Hoffman, Paul. *The Man Who Loved Only Numbers: The Story of Paul Erdös and the Search for Mathematical Truth*. London: Fourth Estate Limited, 1998.
Hopkins, John H. *A Scriptural, Ecclesiastical, and Historical View of Slavery, from the Days of the Patriarch Abraham, to the Nineteenth Century*. 1864. Reprint, New York: Negro Universities Press, 1969.
Hugo, Victor. *Les Misérables*. Translated by Christine Donougher. Kindle ed. London: Penguin, 2013.
Iati, Marisa. "Conversion therapy center founder who sought to turn LGBTQ Christians straight says he's gay, rejects 'cycle of self shame.'" *The Washington Post*, September 5, 2019.
Ivanhoe, Philip, trans. *The Daodejing of Laozi*. Indianapolis, IN: Hackett, 2003.

Jenson, Robert W. *Systematic Theology, Volume 1: The Triune God*. New York: Oxford University Press, 1997.
Keller, Timothy. *The Reason for God: Belief in an Age of Skepticism*. New York: Penguin, 2008.
Khazan, Olga. "The Forgiveness Boost." *The Atlantic* January 28, 2015. http://www.theatlantic.com/health/archive/2015/01/the-forgiveness-boost/384796/.
Kingston, Tom. "Captain who commanded Costa Concordia in cruise disaster that killed 32 begins 16-year prison sentence." *Los Angeles Times* May 12, 2017. https://www.latimes.com/world/europe/la-fg-costa-concordia-20170512-story.html.
Ladin, Dror. "There's So Much We Still Don't Know about the CIA's Torture Program. Here's How the Government Is Keeping the Full Story a Secret." *Time*, February 7, 2020. https://time.com/5779579/cia-torture-secrecy/.
LaPlante, Eve. *Salem Witch Judge: The Life and Repentance of Samuel Sewall*. New York: HarperOne, 2007.
Lee, Harper. *To Kill a Mockingbird*. New York: Warner, 1982.
Leonhard, Robert. *The Art of Maneuver: Maneuver-Warfare Theory and Airland Battle*. Novato, CA: Presidio, 1991.
Levi, Primo. *If This Is a Man and The Truce*. Translated by Stuart Woolf. London: Abacus, 1987.
Lewin, Ronald. *Rommel as Military Commander*. New York: Barnes & Noble, 1998.
Lewis, C. S. *The Problem of Pain*. New York: Macmillan, 1962.
———. *The Screwtape Letters*. Rev. ed. New York: Macmillan, 1982.
Lewis-Williams, David. *Conceiving God: The Cognitive Origin and Evolution of Religion*. London: Thames and Hudson, 2010.
Lieberman, Matthew. *Social: Why Our Brains Are Wired to Connect*. New York: Crown Publishers, 2013.
Loftus, John. *The Outsider Test for Faith: How to Know Which Religion Is True*. New York: Prometheus, 2013.
Lomax, Eric. *The Railway Man: A POW's Searing Account of War, Brutality, and Forgiveness*. New York: W. W. Norton, 2008.
Malkin, Peter, and Harry Stein. *Eichmann in My Hands*. New York: Warner, 1990.
Marshall, Rob, dir. *Chicago*. Los Angeles: Miramax, 2002.
Martin, Dale B. *Sex and the Single Savior: Gender and Sexuality in Biblical Interpretation*. Louisville: Westminster John Knox, 2006.
McLaughlin, Mignon. *The Neurotic's Notebook*. Bobbs-Merrill: Indianapolis, 1963.
McPherson, James M. *Battle Cry of Freedom: The Civil War Era*. New York: Oxford University Press, 1988.
Monteiro, Norma. "Emma Watson UN Speech." *Youtube*. https://www.youtube.com/watch?v=p-iFl4qhBsE.
Morales, Lymari. "Knowing Someone Gay/Lesbian Affects Views of Gay Issues." *Gallup* May 29, 2009. https://news.gallup.com/poll/118931/knowing-someone-gay-lesbian-affects-views-gay-issues.aspx.
Noll, Mark A. *The Civil War as a Theological Crisis*. Chapel Hill, NC: University of North Carolina Press, 2006.
Pareles, Jon. "Pete Seeger, Champion of Folk Music and Social Change, Dies at 94." *The New York Times* January 29, 2014. https://www.nytimes.com/2014/01/29/arts/music/pete-seeger-songwriter-and-champion-of-folk-music-dies-at-94.html.
Philippe, Alexandre, dir. *The People vs. George Lucas*. Denver: Exhibit A Pictures, 2010.
Pinker, Steven. *The Better Angels of Our Nature: Why Violence Has Declined*. New York: Viking, 2011.

Plato. *Euthyphro, Apology, Crito, Phaedo, Phaedrus.* Translated by Harold North Fowler. Cambridge, MA: Harvard University Press, 1914.

Press Association. "J. K. Rowling: Hermione Should Have Married Harry, Not Ron." *The Guardian,* February 2, 2014. https://www.theguardian.com/books/2014/feb/02/jk-rowling-hermione-harry-ron-married.

Prothero, Donald R. *Evolution: What the Fossils Say and Why It Matters.* New York: Columbia University Press, 2007.

Quoidbach, Jordi, Daniel T. Gilbert, and Timothy D. Wilson. "The End of History Illusion." *Science* 339 (January 4, 2013) 96–98.

Radiolab. "Tit for Tat." https://www.wnycstudios.org/podcasts/radiolab/segments/104010-one-good-deed-deserves-another.

Repcheck, Jack. *The Man Who Found Time: James Hutton and the Discovery of the Earth's Antiquity.* Cambridge, MA: Perseus, 2003.

Rodrigues, Luis. "George Carlin - Idiot and Maniac." *YouTube.* https://www.youtube.com/watch?v=XWPCE2tTLZQ.

Rowling, J. K. *Harry Potter and the Deathly Hallows.* New York: Arthur A. Levine, 2007.

Sagan, Carl. *The Demon-Haunted World: Science as a Candle in the Dark.* New York: Random House, 1995.

Sartre, Jean-Paul. *No Exit and Three Other Plays.* New York: Vintage, 1989.

Schreiner, Thomas. "An Interpretation of 1 Timothy 2:9–15: A Dialogue with Scholarship." In *Women in the Church: A Fresh Analysis of 1 Timothy 2:9–15,* edited by Andreas J. Köstenberger, Thomas R. Schreiner, and H. Scott Baldwin, 105–54. Grand Rapids: Baker, 1995.

Schweitzer, Albert. *The Quest of the Historical Jesus: A Critical Study of Its Progress from Reimarus to Wrede.* Translated by W. Montgomery. New York: Macmillan, 1961.

Shepard, Alan, et al. *Moon Shot: The Inside Story of America's Apollo Moon Landings.* Kindle ed. New York: Open Road Media, 2011.

Shults, F. LeRon. *Christology and Science.* Grand Rapids: Eerdmans, 2008.

———. *Iconoclastic Theology: Gilles Deleuze and the Secretion of Atheism.* Edinburgh: Edinburgh University Press, 2014.

———. *On Practicing Safe Sects: Religious Reproduction in Scientific and Philosophical Perspective.* Boston: Brill, 2018.

———. *Reforming the Doctrine of God.* Grand Rapids: Eerdmans, 2005.

———. "Science and Religious Supremacy: Toward a Naturalist Theology of Religions." In *Science and the World's Religions: Religions and Controversies,* edited by Patrick McNamara and Wesley J. Wildman, 3:73–100. Santa Barbara, CA: Praeger, 2012.

———. *Theology after the Birth of God: Atheist Conceptions in Cognition and Culture.* New York: Palgrave Macmillan, 2014.

———. "Theology after Pandora: The Real Scandal of the Evangelical Mind (and Culture)." In *Revisioning, Renewing, Rediscovering the Triune Center: Essays in Honor of Stanley J. Grenz,* edited by Derek J. Tidball et al., 361–81. Eugene, OR: Cascade, 2014.

Siegel, Ethan. "Dark Energy Renders 97% of the Galaxies in Our Observable Universe Permanently Unreachable." *Forbes* June 8, 2015. https://www.forbes.com/sites/ethansiegel/2015/06/08/dark-energy-renders-97-of-the-galaxies-in-our-observable-universe-permanently-unreachable/.

Smith, Nick. "Sorry But Not Sorry." *Aeon* October 15, 2014. https://aeon.co/essays/how-the-public-apology-became-a-tool-of-power-and-privilege.

Solberg, Mary M. *A Church Undone: Documents from the German Christian Faith Movement, 1932–40.* Minneapolis: Fortress, 2015.

Solzhenitsyn, Aleksandr. *The Gulag Archipelago*. Abridged by Edward Ericson. New York: Perennial Classics, 2002.

Sun Tzu. *The Art of War*. Edited by James Clavell. New York: Delacorte, 1983.

Taibbi, Matt. "Cruel and Unusual Punishment: The Shame of Three Strikes Laws." *Rolling Stone* March 27, 2013. https://www.rollingstone.com/politics/politics-news/cruel-and-unusual-punishment-the-shame-of-three-strikes-laws-92042/.

Tarico, Valerie. "Surprise! Atheist Marriages May Last Longer Than Christian Ones." *AlterNet* October 30, 2013. https://www.alternet.org/2013/10/surprise-atheist-marriages-may-last-longer-christian-ones/.

Tavris, Carol, and Elliot Aronson. *Mistakes Were Made (but Not by Me): Why We Justify Foolish Beliefs, Bad Decisions, and Hurtful Acts*. Orlando: Harcourt, 2007.

Taylor, Chris. *How Star Wars Conquered the Universe: The Past, Present, and Future of a Multibillion Dollar Franchise*. New York: Basic Books, 2014.

Thornwell, James H. *The Collected Writings of James Henley Thornwell, vol. IV: Ecclesiastical*. 1873. Reprint, Edinburgh: Banner of Truth, 1974.

Tolkien, J. R. R. *The Letters of J. R. R. Tolkien*. Kindle ed. Edited by Humphrey Carpenter. New York: Houghton Mifflin Harcourt, 1981.

Tolstoy, Leo. *Anna Karenina*. Translated by Rosamund Bartlett. Oxford: Oxford University Press, 2014.

Tomcat. "Atheists for Jesus: A Richard Dawkins Essay." December 11, 2006. https://www.rationalresponders.com/atheists_for_jesus_a_richard_dawkins_essay.

Tutu, Desmond. *No Future without Forgiveness*. Kindle ed. New York: Doubleday, 1999.

Tyson, Neil deGrasse. "The good thing about Science." Twitter post. April 11, 2021, 3:47 a.m. https://twitter.com/neiltyson/status/1381197292728942595.

Uys, Jamie, dir. *The Gods Must Be Crazy*. Johannesburg, South Africa: Ster-Kinekor, 1980.

Wachowski, Lana, and Lilly Wachowski, dirs. *The Matrix*. Burbank, CA: Warner Bros., 1999.

Weschler, Lawrence. "A Rare, Personal Look at Oliver Sacks's Early Career." *Vanity Fair* April 28, 2015. https://www.vanityfair.com/culture/2015/04/oliver-sacks-autobiography-before-cancer.

Wikipedia. "All models are wrong." https://en.wikipedia.org/wiki/All_models_are_wrong.

———. "List of Cognitive Biases." https://en.wikipedia.org/wiki/List_of_cognitive_biases.

———. "The Search for Signs of Intelligent Life in the Universe." https://en.wikipedia.org/wiki/The_Search_for_Signs_of_Intelligent_Life_in_the_Universe.

Williams, Neil H. *The Maleness of Jesus: Is It Good News for Women?* Eugene, OR: Cascade, 2011.

Williams, Rowan. *Tokens of Trust: An Introduction to Christian Belief*. Louisville: Westminster John Knox, 2007.

Winston, Kimberly. "Leading Atheist, Accused of Sexual Misconduct, Speaks Out." *Washington Post* September 6, 2018. https://www.washingtonpost.com/news/acts-of-faith/wp/2018/09/06/americas-leading-atheist-accused-of-sexual-misconduct-speaks-out/.

Wright, Lawrence. *Going Clear: Scientology, Hollywood, and the Prison of Belief*. New York: Alfred Knopf, 2013.

Yancey, Philip. *What's So Amazing about Grace?* Grand Rapids: Zondervan, 1997.

www.ingramcontent.com/pod-product-compliance
Lightning Source LLC
Chambersburg PA
CBHW051934160426
43198CB00013B/2151